Caithness
and
Sutherland
40 Coast and Country Walks

D1634949

The author and publisher have made every effort to ensure that the information in this publication is accurate, and accept no responsibility whatsoever for any loss, injury or inconvenience experienced by any person or persons whilst using this book.

published by
pocket mountains ltd
6 Church Wynd, Bo'ness EH51 0AN
pocketmountains.com

ISBN: 978-1-9070250-8-2

Printed in Poland

Introduction

The remarkable landscapes of Caithness and Sutherland make up the northernmost part of the Scottish mainland. Whilst Highland areas like Loch Lomond, Glencoe and the Cairngorms are familiar to thousands, far fewer make the effort to travel so much further north. Those who do receive their reward: there is no other place that looks anything like this.

Apart from the eastern coastal fringe, the defining character of the region is its lack of people. The interior holds vast, empty tracts of moorland and bog with countless lochans. The mountains may be lower than those further south, but they rise abruptly and often in spectacular isolation. The coastline, deeply indented to the west and north, is decorated with an array of deserted beaches – undoubtedly the finest in mainland Britain. Whilst at first glance, this landscape may seem suited only to the most hardy adventurers, it is packed with hidden nooks, crannies and undiscovered oases – this is a wonderland for the more moderate walker too.

Using this guide

This guide contains 40 short to moderate walks, most of which can be undertaken in half a day, which explore all parts of this vast area. Whilst some are on prepared paths, many others are not and a number cross boggy, rocky or occasionally steep ground. The weather, whilst not as wet as the West Highlands, is extremely changeable, with strong winds a particular feature. Always remember that this is a wild landscape and help is sometimes far away. Most of the walks require waterproof footwear and clothing. Whilst a sketch map accompanies each route, walkers should also carry an OS map to aid navigation and find the shortest route to safety. More challenging walks, such as Dunnet Head or the Eas a'Chual Aluinn, are best tackled by experienced hillwalkers. Due to the varied landscape, very few walks are suitable for all-terrain baby buggies; if a route is appropriate, this is highlighted at the start of the description. Many of the routes are suitable for well-clad families, however, with features such as beaches or ruined castles to occupy children.

As might be expected, public transport is limited. The only railway line runs from Wick and Thurso, crossing the bogs of the Flow Country before continuing down the east coast to eventually link to Inverness. Bus services are good along the A9 and as far across as Thurso, but those further west are very infrequent, though there is a daily service from Inverness to Durness.

Access and dogs

The Land Reform (Scotland) Act 2003 gave walkers the right of access over most Scottish land away from residential buildings. With this right comes responsibilities, as set out in the Scottish Outdoor Access Code. These essentially require respect for other land users and responsible access, especially on farmed and grazing land. In particular, dogs should be kept on tight leads during the

3

spring and early summer to stop them disturbing groundnesting birds and farm livestock. They should also be kept well away from sheep with lambs at all times. Deer stalking takes place on the hills between 1 July and 20 October, but this should not usually conflict with the walks described in this guide as long as you stick to the recommended routes. Ticks and midges can sometimes be a hazard during the summer months. Take precautions such as covering up, wearing light-coloured clothing, using insect repellent and checking for and removing ticks daily.

History

Though so far from the main centres of population today, Caithness and Sutherland both have a very long history. In particular, Caithness (together with neighbouring Orkney) is unmatched for its range of well-preserved prehistoric remains. The massive Grey Cairns of Camster are the finest bronze age chambered cairns in this area, with other examples visited on these walks. Much later, but still impressive, are the iron age brochs, defensive round towers with double curtain walls into which the settlers could retreat with their animals when under attack. There are more than one hundred scattered across the region, from Clachtoll Beach in the west to Carn Liath in the east.

The name Sutherland, meaning 'South Land', is a reminder that for many centuries this region fell under Norwegian rule, with the headquarters in Orkney. The Norse influence reached its peak in the 11th century; after their eventual defeat, the area was ruled by the Earls of Caithness, chiefs of Clan Sinclair. Evidence of this period can be seen in the string of ruined castles along the Caithness coastline, including Sinclair Girnigoe and Old Wick, as well as the Castle of Mey, in more recent times restored as a residence by the Queen Mother.

It was the defeat of the Jacobite rebellion far to the south at Culloden in 1746 which began the separation of the clan chiefs from their people that was to eventually prove so disastrous for the area. By the 19th century, the chiefs were looking jealously on the lavish lifestyles of the great landowners further south, and the demand for wool sparked by the Industrial Revolution gave them the opportunity to begin extracting great wealth from their own landholdings. They began to evict the people from their lands to make way for sheep. The crofters were forced to make new homes along the barren, windswept coastline – or to flee Scotland in search of a better life overseas. Evidence of this cruel episode can be seen throughout the region today, and not just in the emptiness of the straths. Walks such as that at Rosal in Strathnaver explore the remains of the old settlements and productive lands which the crofters were forced to abandon, whilst others such as Badbea visit the ruins of the desperate villages that they built once they reached the coast. These stand in stark contrast to the magnificent fairytale opulence of Dunrobin Castle, much of it ating to the same period – built as a home or the Dukes of Sutherland themselves.

Natural history

In 2004, the western part of Sutherland was designated Scotland's first European geopark in recognition of its fascinating geology. The older layers of rock (the Lewisian gneiss that covers much of the surface is amongst the oldest in the world) were driven over the top of younger rocks by a great movement of the earth known as the Moine Thrust. Understanding of the Thrust became key in the development of modern tectonic theory – that the crust of the earth is made up of a series of moving plates. It is this part of Sutherland which has become famed for its isolated peaks or inselbergs – island mountains – rising steeply above otherwise flat moors. Further east, the sandstone and thin siltstone that make up the geology of Caithness drove a key part of its economy, splitting easily into regular sheets or flagstones which make an ideal roofing and building material. Many of the field boundaries here are constructed from lines of upright flagstones, seldom seen elsewhere.

This area also has a rich flora and fauna, with important seabird colonies scattered all around the coastline, among them puffins, great skuas, razorbills, guillemots and kittiwakes. Several walks offer excellent bird-spotting opportunities, especially Handa Island, Dunnet Head and Duncansby Head which all have large and important colonies. Inland, the great peat bogs of the Flow Country, covering almost half of the area, are a vital habitat, constituting 13 percent of the world's blanket bogs. They are renowned for their plant and birdlife; species to watch for include hen harrier, merlin, greenshank (66 percent of the European population live here), dunlin and golden plover. The Dubh Lochan trail on the bogs is managed by the RSPB who own the Forsinard reserve here.

Caithness and Sutherland today

Traditional sporting estates still own vast parts of Sutherland, and deer stalking, shooting and forestry remain important parts of the economy. With its legendary salmon rivers, fishing, too, is a major draw, whilst in the southeastern corner golf is a key money-spinner.

The controversial Dounreay nuclear power plant closed in 1994, but its significance to the economy of Caithness endures, as more than 2000 people are employed in decommissioning, due to be completed in 2025. In recent years, the drive towards renewable energy has seen the construction of large-scale windfarms, though the most sensitive and scenic areas in the west have been unaffected. Many more turbines are planned, and the issue has caused a painful split in the usual alliance between environmental campaigners and landscape and wildlife conservationists.

Tourism continues to grow, particularly along the western and northern coastlines. Scotland has positioned itself as Europe's wildlife capital, and this area has so much to offer in natural history and culture as well as its superlative landscape.

Assynt boasts some of Scotland's most remarkable scenery. The sublime rocky coastline is dotted with magnificent sandy beaches. The few glens are narrow, sparsely populated, twisting and dotted with birches. The moorland is speckled with countless glittering lochans. And rising above all of this is a series of bizarre individual mountains, some of which look so improbable as to make the first-time visitor doubt the evidence of his eyes. It is

little wonder that the great poet Norman MacCaig spent so much time here or placed it at the heart of so much of his work.

The fishing village of Lochinver – still bustling with working boats – is the main centre of population, serving a series of tiny communities strung out along the coastline. Here, you'll find shops, places to stay and eat and a celebrated pottery, not to mention the extravagant sugar-loaf outline of Suilven looming behind.

...ssynt

The Bone Caves

Distance 4.5km **Time** 1 hour 45
Terrain mostly clear path, narrow where it
crosses a steep slope; slippery inside the
caves **Map** OS Explorer 442 **Access** bus
(67A) from Ullapool and Lochinver; also
on postbus (123) route

**Head up an empty glen to visit a
fascinating group of caves. Try to imagine
the distant past – an era when lynx,
reindeer and (possibly) polar bear roamed
across these slopes. The remains of these
beasts and other animals have all been
found in the caves, though nowadays in
summer you are more likely to find small
children crawling between the chambers
than an animal hunted by our ancestors.**

The car park for the Bone Caves is signed
on the east side of the A837 between
Elphin and Inchnadamph. Start through

the gate, walking past a building and alo[ng]
a path that follows the course of the Allt
nan Uamh, the 'River of the Caves'. Just
beyond a waterfall, the path begins its
gentle climb, passing a large spring on th[e]
left where an underground watercourse
emerges into daylight.

Being limestone, this part of Assynt
provides the most extensive cave systems
in Scotland and has long been a magnet f[or]
archaeologists and cavers. The caves were
formed when water from a glacier filling
the glen began to dissolve the limestone
bedrock more than 200,000 years ago.

The caves soon come into sight on the
far side of the glen, across the usually dry
riverbed. At a junction, stay on the left si[de]
of the river to carry on up the glen beyon[d]
the caves. The route eventually crosses th[e]
riverbed and heads up a dry valley on the

ar side. The path here is well made and climbs to a clear right-hand turning for the final ascent back to the caves. Take care on the narrow section as it crosses the steep grassy slope, particularly if the ground is wet.

Soon, you'll reach the first of the series of four caves. There is a tiny passage, only wide enough for a small child, connecting Reindeer and Bone Caves. The first excavations here took place in 1889 and revealed animal bones thought to date back to over 45,000 years ago. Further digs in 1925 found a tooth of a bear and pieces of reindeer antler. The following year, the first human remains were found. Archaeologists think that whilst the caves

may have been used as a temporary hunting base, they were not lived in permanently – although they may have been used as a burial site. The human bones found in the caves were more than 4500 years old. Since then, many more animal remains have been found, including wildcat, lynx, arctic lemming, arctic fox, black and brown bears and possibly a polar bear. This last find has been dated as being more than 18,800 years old: the mind boggles at the thought of polar bears roaming this landscape during the last ice age.

To return, take the path to the left which drops steeply into the glen and crosses the riverbed to rejoin the outward path.

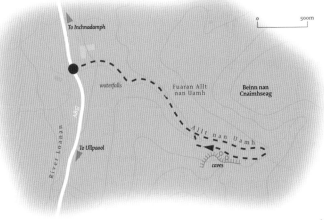

Inchnadamph Caves

Distance 7km Time 2 hours 30
Terrain track and path, can be wet
underfoot; extreme care is needed near
the cave openings Map OS Explorer 442
Access bus (67A) from Ullapool or
Lochinver, also on postbus (123) route

Visit the gaping entrances of the largest cave system in Scotland. Part of the walk follows the Munro-baggers' route to Conival and Ben More Assynt, so you may find the route shared with keen hillwalkers as well as speleologists.

Start from the public car park near the Inchnadamph Hotel and walk a very short distance north along the main road to cross a bridge, before turning right onto a track. Pass an imposing white building: once the manse, it now provides hostel accommodation. Go through a gate, passing an information board. The track now leads uphill, crossing the Allt Poll an Droighinn; it is possible to shortcut across one zigzag via a path before rejoining the track further on.

It is not long before you pass the isolated cottage at Glenbain and the route levels off as the track becomes fainter. Where it forks take the right-hand branch, crossing the river on a footbridge before inclining uphill. After 500m, the entrance to the first cave system is reached. Uamh an Tartair is Gaelic for 'The Cave of the Roaring' and is an impressive sight. A yawning hole rent

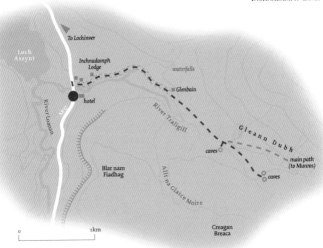

To Lochinver

Loch Assynt

Inchnadamph Lodge

waterfalls

Glenbain

hotel

River Traligill

River Loanan

Gleann Dubh

caves

main path (to Munros)

caves

Blar nam Fiadhag

Allt na Glaice Moire

Creagan Breaca

0   1km

n the ground has a river cascading into
it from a higher pothole – do not attempt
to enter. The caves were excavated in the
20th century and, as well as animal
remains, human bones were discovered,
leading archaeologists to believe they were
once inhabited.

Follow the path to the left to reach the
large but more amenable entrance of
Uamh an Uisge, 'Cave of the Water'. Here,
the water can clearly be heard rushing
somewhere underground. With great care,
the cave entrance area can be explored
with a torch; there is a second chamber
accessible below a low arch. Beyond the
arch, the cave becomes very dangerous
and must be left to those with proper
equipment and experience. Like many
limestone cave systems, it can very
quickly fill with water and even the

entrance area can flood at times.

When blinking eyes have adjusted to the
light back outside, enjoy great views back
down the glen to Loch Assynt and the
distinctive peaks of Quinag. Before
heading back, it is possible to visit the
upper pothole from which the water flows
down into the Uamh an Tartair. Climb
above the Uamh an Uisge and then head
across to the right. The deep chasm of the
upper pothole is unprotected, so again
keep a safe distance.

Walk back along the path to the
footbridge. Before returning, there is one
final detour to make; take the path along
the river to the left to reach a large cliff
where the water disappears into the mouth
of a cavern with a small gorge below.
Return to the main path and retrace your
steps to Inchnadamph.

◀ Approach to Inchnadamph Caves

11

Leitir Easaidh

Distance **2.5km** Time **45 minutes**
Terrain **all-abilities path suitable for many buggies and wheelchairs**
Map **OS Explorer 442**
Access **no public transport to start**

An easy walk with fabulous views, passing three lochs where you may catch sight of black-throated divers, golden eagles or even otters. The path has been carefully graded to make it suitable for buggies and wheelchairs, and there are plenty of seats, shelters and a quirky thatched composting toilet on the way.

The Leitir Easaidh car park is signed from the A837 between Inchnadamph and Lochinver. There is a map of the trail and information on a board near the start. Go through the gate and soon you'll see some small buildings. Take the path branching to the right to reach these and visit the shore of Loch Leitir Easaidh. The thatched hut is a solar- and wind-powered composting toilet and just beyond it is a shelter and a pier for anglers. Over the water, the massive wall of rock that seems to rise almost vertically from the moors is Quinag, a popular target for hillwalkers, admittedly usually tackled via a less forbidding approach.

Return to the trail and keep left at the next fork. When the path branches again, go right for a short detour over a bridge to a picnic area and the lochside. Back on the main trail, the shore of the second body of water, Loch na h-Innse Fraoich, is soon gained. There is another shelter, toilet and

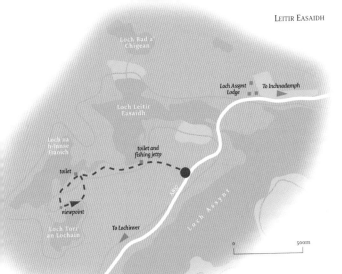

boat jetty here. At the fork, keep right to complete a loop with fabulous views of the wilds of Assynt.

While the scenery has barely changed for centuries, the management of the land has recently undergone a seismic upheaval. In June 2005, the local community used new access laws to buy out two local estates, following in the footsteps of an earlier buy out on a nearby estate. The land includes the mountains of Suilven, Canisp, Cul Beag and Cul Mor and the adjoining mass of lochans, wild and crofted landscape – over 44,000 acres in total. Whilst it took an act of the Scottish parliament and fundraising on a massive and international scale to achieve the buy-out, the aims have been in the minds of local people for a very long time.

In 1886, the Lochinver branch of the Highland Land League had demanded the restoration to the people of the deer forest of Glencanisp 'where there is plenty of provision for ourselves and our families. It extends twenty-one miles ... and the land of our fathers lying waste'. The Assynt Foundation now manages the land with the aim of ensuring a viable and sustainable community can live in the area whilst also protecting the natural environment.

Climb very gently, bearing right at a fork and then left to reach a viewpoint. Here, you are looking across Loch Torr an Lochain to the remarkable outline of Suilven. Return to the main track, keeping right at both junctions to retrace the outward route.

Falls of Kirkaig

Distance 7km **Time** 3 hours
Terrain good path up the glen; final
descent to the falls is steep and dangerous
– great care needed **Map** OS Explorer 442
Access nearest bus stop is at Lochinver,
3.5km away on minor roads

What the Falls of Kirkaig lack in height
they make up for with their great power in
all but the driest of weather, making a
grand climax to an excursion up the fine
wooded glen. After the walk, you can
enjoy a well-earned cup of tea at Achins,
reputedly Scotland's remotest bookshop.

Inverkirkaig is a small coastal settlement
around 4km south of Lochinver; the minor
road then heads inland beside the River
Kirkaig and there is a car park just before
the bridge. Two tarred tracks lead upriver
from here – the higher one heading to the
bookshop and café, and the lower being
the start of the walk. Pass a memorial to
Norman MacCaig, an Edinburgh man
whose poetry did so much to bring this
stunning area to a wider public. MacCaig's
mother was a Highlander and he spent
much of his time away from the capital
either here at Inverkirkaig or at Achmelvich

further up the coast. His poetry is full of a deep love of Assynt, its landscape, its wildlife and its people.

Branch right onto a footpath after 250m, soon passing through an iron gate to enter birch woodland. The path descends to run alongside the river, a beautiful spot with steep woodland rising off to either side. Pass through a kissing gate and climb gently as the glen begins to narrow. Emerge from the birches onto wilder heather moorland, continuing high above the glen floor. Cul Mor and Cul Beag soon come into view, as well as the jagged ridge of Stac Pollaidh over to the right.

Eventually Suilven appears ahead, its flat-topped but vertically-flanked summit of Caisteal Liath appearing like a thimble.

After 3km, the path forks and a sign indicates the start of a path on the right which descends to the falls. This inclines gently down towards the gorge at first, but soon reaches a very steep slope. From here, the path is poor and great care is needed to make the final very rocky descent – a slip could be fatal. The best viewing spot for the falls is about three quarters of the way down. The Falls of Kirkaig are 20m high, which may be tiny compared to the Eas a'Chual Aluinn, but the volume of water passing over the falls usually make for spectacular viewing. Return up the steep slope to regain the main path. The return to Inverkirkaig is by the outward route.

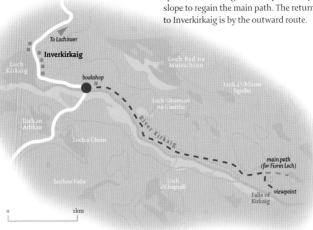

Glencanisp and River Inver

Distance 7.5km Time 3 hours
Terrain small but clear riverside and
moorland paths Map OS Explorer 442
Access bus (67A) from Ullapool to
Lochinver

**Soak up the fabulous Assynt views on this
varied walk from Lochinver. The route
takes in a fine stretch of riverside, a
moorland crossing and an attractive loch,
all with dramatic mountain backdrops.**

Lochinver is a small community
dependent on tourism, crofting and
fishing. It is not uncommon for the voices
in the Culag bar of an evening to be a wide
mix of locals, fishing boat workers from
Eastern Europe and further afield, English
incomers, and enthusiastic German, Dutch
and Belgian hillwalkers. Backed by the

sugar-loaf mountain of Suilven and
boasting a café with the best selection of
home-made pies you'll ever see, Lochinver
makes a great base for touring the area.
Begin from the waterfront car park near the
church. From here, walk north along the
pavement, passing the turning for
Baddidarach. Keep an eye out for a gate to
the right, which is the start of the riverside
path, signposted 'Glencanisp Loop'.

The River Inver tumbles down from the
hills over small falls and between boulders
on its way to the sea at Lochinver. Follow it
upstream, passing through a gate and
keeping right when small paths lead to
salmon fishing points over to the left. A
number of piers and small weirs have been
constructed to provide resting and

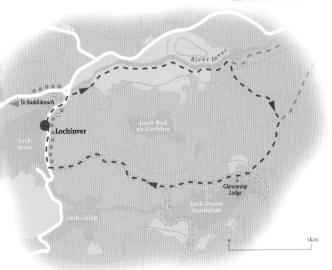

spawning areas for the salmon; they are used by fly fisherman during the season. If you are lucky, you might catch a glimpse of a salmon leaping as it makes its way upstream to return to its spawning area.

Higher up, the river becomes wider and more sedate. Continue on the main path, ignoring branches off to the left as you accompany the river round a bend to reach a small gate marking the start of the open moors. Ahead in the distance lies the impressive mountain wall of Quinag. As the path nears a birchwood beside the water, look carefully for a path peeling off to the right. This takes you away from the river on a rising course through the heather, passing the remains of settlements whose inhabitants were

forcibly evicted during the Highland Clearances. Eventually, you come to a metal gate and, after passing through this, turn right onto a wider path which climbs over a low pass before heading down towards Loch Druim Suardalain.

After reaching the woods, the path meets a track at an old iron shed. Follow this to the right to pass Glencanisp Lodge. Now owned by the Assynt Foundation following the community buy-out in 2005, this grand building is available for group hire. Join the driveway to the lodge for an amble alongside the loch. Looking back, there are classic views of Canisp and Suilven. The driveway eventually becomes a minor public road and leads back into Lochinver and the start point.

Achmelvich Beach

Distance **6km** Time **2 hours**
Terrain **good coastal path**
Map **OS Explorer 442** Access **twice daily
bus (67A) from Ullapool to Achmelvich**

By a trick of the light, the sea at
Achmelvich Bay can look almost tropical.
The perfect beach is the reward for the
tortuous single-track road that winds
through the rocky landscape to reach the
coast. The area has a loyal band of regular
visitors, and a sandcastle competition and
mini-olympics are organised during the
summer months. Note that in summer
dogs are banned from the beach.

From the car park at Achmelvich, follow
the track signed for Alltan'abradhan,
passing through a gate as you climb. Turn
left onto a signed path as a house comes
into view. After meandering through the
rocky landscape overlooking the lovely
beach and blue sea, pass to the left of the
house and continue round the coast on
springy turf. At a stone wall, go through
the small gate and down to another wall
before climbing up and over the next rise.
Just before the road, turn left and then
swing right at a sign before some cottages.
Cross the road and take a track uphill
towards a modern house. Follow the path
to the left of the house and down to a
burn, crossing by stepping stones. Situated
here is the ruined mill of Alltan'abradhan,
the old mill stones once driven by a paddle

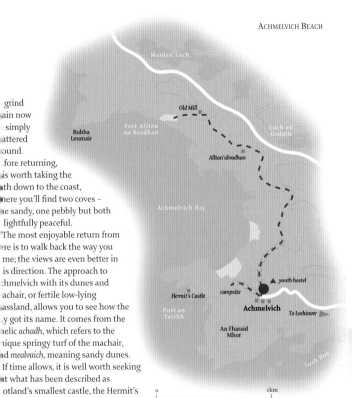

grind
ain now
simply
attered
ound.

fore returning,
is worth taking the
th down to the coast,
here you'll find two coves –
e sandy, one pebbly but both
lightfully peaceful.

The most enjoyable return from
re is to walk back the way you
me; the views are even better in
is direction. The approach to
hmelvich with its dunes and
achair, or fertile low-lying
assland, allows you to see how the
y got its name. It comes from the
elic *achadh*, which refers to the
nique springy turf of the machair,
d *mealvaich*, meaning sandy dunes.

If time allows, it is well worth seeking
t what has been described as
otland's smallest castle, the Hermit's
astle, which lies on the far side of the
ninsula that shelters the bay. To reach it,
alk to the Achmelvich campsite and turn
ft in front of the shop to head towards
e far end, where a gate and stile lead
nto An Fharaid Bheag. Aim directly west,
eping high to avoid the worst of the
kward, slabby terrain, and soon the tiny
ructure can be seen perched on a rock
verlooking a small inlet. Constructed in
ncrete, the castle was reportedly built in

the 1950s or early '60s by an English
architect, David Scott, who only spent one
night in it before leaving the area for good.
Presumably the planning officer did not
venture this far from the road! The tiny
windows and door have long been
removed, leaving a gloomy interior, with
compensation in the fabulous setting and
beautiful sunsets.

Beach at Achmelvich

Clachtoll Beach and Broch

Distance 3km **Time** 1 hour 15
Terrain springy turf, rocky shore, minor
road **Map** OS Explorer 442 **Access** nearest
bus (67A) stops at Drumbeg Post Office,
1.5km away on minor road

**Clachtoll Beach appears gleaming white
beside a turquoise sea, even on the dullest
of days. This walk leaves the campsite and
beachcombers behind to explore the
nearby coast and visit the remains of a
broch – an iron age defensive structure.**

To reach the Clachtoll Beach car park,
follow the signs to the campsite. Here, the
rangers' hut gives information on the local
area and the wildlife that can often be seen
from this route. These coastal waters are
popular with a range of marine mammals,
including dolphins, minke whales and the
second largest fish in the world, the
plankton-eating basking shark, which ca[?]
weigh up to 19 tons.

As the path approaches the beach, bear
right to climb a stile and aim for the tiny
white building. This was a salmon-nettin[?]
bothy, but has been restored as an
information centre about this industry.
Closed in 1994, the Clachtoll netting
station once drew more than 100 salmon
per day from these waters using nets
strung out from poles on the beach, whic[?]
were pulled in as the tide turned. The
fishermen would have used the bothy as
their temporary home during the season
which ran from February to August. The
poles outside were used to dry the nets
and an ice house – the remains still visib[?]
– stored the ice needed to pack the fish
into crates and barrels for their journey
south to market.

Go through the gate and, just before reaching another, head to the right to go through a walkers' gate giving access to the Rev Norman MacLeod memorial. Born in 1780, Norman MacLeod was brought up in Assynt but studied in Aberdeen and Edinburgh before returning to the area as a teacher and lay preacher. His theological conflicts with the local minister led to his departure and later emigration to Nova Scotia. Here, he joined a community of Highland immigrants whose numbers continued to swell, fuelled by the Clearances, and MacLeod found a ready audience for his strict interpretation of God's word. Eventually ordained in New York, the Rev MacLeod's followers became known as Normanites, a large Gaelic-speaking, Sabbath-observing community based at St Ann's, Cape Breton Island, where today the school remains the centre for Gaelic learning in Canada. The Rev Macleod later moved on to Australia and then New Zealand, pushed into further emigration, along with more than 800 of his followers, by the hardships caused by potato blight.

From the memorial, follow the stone wall to another gate and walk uphill and along the grassy coast, keeping well clear of the rock slabs that plunge into the sea. The massive pile of stones visible ahead is the remains of Clachtoll Broch, a double-

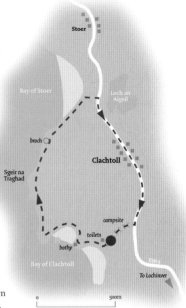

walled iron age building probably used for hiding people and livestock at times of attack. The entrance was on the far side, but the structure has been fenced off to protect it from damage.

The easiest way back is to retrace your outward route. Alternatively, you can continue along the fence over rough ground to cross boulders before reaching the end of the field near the Bay of Stoer. Turn right here to reach the road, and then follow it to the right until a sign indicates the way back along the drive into the car park.

Point of Stoer

Distance 7km **Time** 3 hours
Terrain rough pathless coast, often wet
underfoot, care needed near cliff edge
Map OS Explorer 442 **Access** nearest bus
(67A) stops at Clashnessie, 4km away

This more demanding coastal walk is
well worth the effort, rewarded by
fantastic cliff formations, far-reaching
views and an opportunity for some whale
or dolphin spotting. The Old Man himself
is a towering sea stack, an inspirational
challenge to rock climbers which instils
awe in walkers. Binoculars are a must for
this walk, to watch climbers on the stack,
the seabirds they share the cliffs with and,
hopefully, the odd marine mammal.

Start from the car park at the end of the
minor road leading to Stoer Lighthouse,
just off the B869 north of Lochinver. Follow
the grassy path signed for Old Man of
Stoer. Head uphill, keeping parallel with

the coast and soon you will be able to loo
down on the lighthouse. The lighthouse
was built in 1870 by the Stevenson family
who had a virtual monopoly on lighthous
design in Scotland. The light has a range o
39km and is now fully automated, with th
old lightkeeper's cottages owned by the
National Trust for Scotland.

The path gets fainter but also drier
underfoot. Detour inland to cross a deep
grassy gully before continuing around th
coast. After passing Cirean Geardail, a
massive rock which projects bravely out
into the sea, the Old Man of Stoer comes
into view ahead.

After passing the highest point of the
cliffs, the route descends steeply to a
grassy area directly above the Old
Man. Whilst at the famous
Old Man of Hoy in Orkney
the sea never totally
surrounds the base,

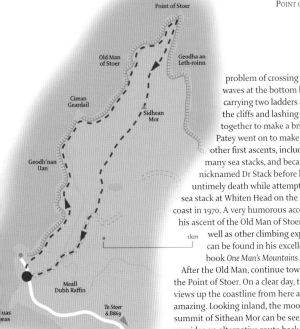

problem of crossing the waves at the bottom by carrying two ladders across the cliffs and lashing them together to make a bridge. Patey went on to make many other first ascents, including many sea stacks, and became nicknamed Dr Stack before his untimely death while attempting a sea stack at Whiten Head on the north coast in 1970. A very humorous account of his ascent of the Old Man of Stoer, as well as other climbing exploits, can be found in his excellent book *One Man's Mountains*.

After the Old Man, continue towards the Point of Stoer. On a clear day, the views up the coastline from here are amazing. Looking inland, the moorland summit of Sithean Mor can be seen; this provides an alternative route back with easier going, despite the extra ascent. Head directly up the broad slope to eventually reach the trig point and cairn. Here, the views are even more spectacular with the Trotternish peninsula, home to another of Patey's first ascents, the Old Man of Storr, often visible.

Follow the faint path, aiming to the right of the mast and keeping left of a small hillock with a cairn on it to avoid an area of bog. Soon, you'll meet the track which leads up to the mast. Turn right to descend past the remains of a radar station and return to the start.

climbers attempting the Old Man of Stoer are definitely in for either a dangerous soaking or a vertigo-inducing Tyrolean traverse across a fixed rope to the starting point for the climb. In 1953, the Scottish Mountaineering Club published its *Northern Highlands* guide, describing the stack as, 'evidently quite unclimbable'. Scottish climber Tom Patey, a GP based in Ullapool at the time, took up the challenge and was the first to reach the top of this 67m sandstone stack in 1966. He solved the

◀ The Old Man of Stoer

Eas a' Chual Aluinn

Distance 10km **Time** 5 hours
Terrain challenging and exposed walk, very rough going and wet in places; extreme care is needed near the top
Map OS Explorer 442 **Access** in summer, Tim Dearman Coaches runs a daily service from Inverness to Durness which can stop here, leaving just enough time to complete the walk – if you hurry

Experience a typically wild part of the Assynt hinterland on this tough trek to the top of Britain's highest waterfall. It crosses rocky heather moorland dotted with numerous lochan to reach the best viewpoint for the falls, which drop 200m into the glen below. Fatal accidents have occurred at the top, so take great care.

This walk crosses very wild terrain; navigation skills and hillwalking gear are needed as the weather can change quickly. Begin from the parking area at the sharp bend on the A894 between Kylesku and the Lochinver junction; it's near the north end of Loch na Gainmhich, about 4km south of Unapool. Follow a section of the old road uphill from the car park and then head across the bogs towards the outflow of the loch. There is no real alternative to this wet start to the walk, but the path does soon improve. Cross the outflow on stepping stones, taking the opportunity to glance left down the small gorge, before aiming directly uphill on the far side to gain a path part way up the slope to the right: this is easier than staying at the water's edge.

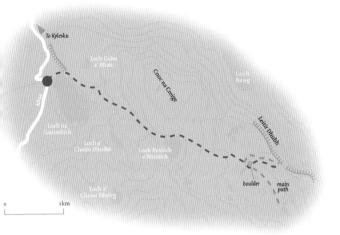

The path runs parallel to the loch before climbing steadily towards the Bealach 'Bhuirich. From here, the walk becomes a wilderness experience of bare rocky knolls and lochans, with the larger Assynt peaks also visible. Pass alongside Loch Bealach 'Bhuirich and then climb to the highest point on the walk at 450m. The subsequent descent winds between outcrops of Lewisian gneiss – among the oldest rocks on the planet.

After a steep section, you meet the main burn. Although it is possible to continue on this side of the water to the lip of the waterfall, it is very difficult to see the falls from there and trying to do so can be very hazardous. Instead, cross the water (which may not be possible if it is in spate) and turn left to descend by a small path. Another 500m brings you to a spot just above the lip of the falls. Do not drop down to the lip but take the path bearing right, keeping close to the cliff edge until a rough descent to a level area slightly lower than the general moorland brings you to a viewpoint looking back to the falls on the left. Here, most of the 200m cascade can be seen, backed by Loch Glencoul, with more distant views of an almost equally dramatic waterfall across the glen.

Britain's highest waterfall could almost come with the additional tag of being the most inaccessible or hard to see, as its full glory is not easily revealed. Even the boat trips from Kylesku cannot get close, and it is necessary to peer through binoculars, so this walk probably does offer the best opportunity for many visitors. The return route is by the same path – the uphill section may feel more strenuous on the way back, but the fabulous views should help to keep you going.

◀ Loch Bealach a'Bhuirich

The map shows the following labeled locations:

Cape Wrath

Whiten Head

⑥

Durness

⑤ ⑦ ⑧

④

Kinlochbervie

Tong

Loch Eriboll

Loch Hope

③

②

① Scourie

Loch More

Kylestrome

Loch Naver

Loch Assynt

Lochinver

The *Ultima Thule* of mainland Britain, this is one of the wildest, barest, rockiest and emptiest of places. Nonetheless, when the sun does shine – which is more often than you might expect – there can be few locations on earth to match its stunning beauty. All around the coast, often bounded by cliffs, are the most spectacular beaches – wide, sweeping arcs of perfect sand, set off by the harshness of the hinterland.

Settlements of any size are limited. Scourie is a former fishing village with a shop and campsite, Kinlochbervie is a busy port for the landing of white fish, but has only a few houses, whilst Durness on the north coast has become the main centre. Adjacent is Balnakeil, a former RAF base which is now home to a craft village and a fine bookshop and café. The furthest corner of all is Cape Wrath, which requires some determination to reach – the journey is by passenger ferry across the Kyle of Durness followed by an 18km minibus ride across the eerie landscape of the Parph.

The Far North West

Scourie Point

Distance **3km** Time **1 hour**
Terrain **faint, rough path**
Map **OS Explorer 445** Access **bus (806/805) from Durness and Lairg to Scourie**

Starting from Scourie Beach, enjoy a stunning and supremely peaceful walk out to the headland. The going underfoot is rough but is rewarded by fabulous views along the coast and out to sea.

Scourie is a small crofting community, much swelled in the summer months by visitors. Originally a stronghold of the Clan MacKay, the laird's fortified house was enlarged in the 1840s to become a coaching inn, and is now the Scourie Hotel. The area bore the brunt of the Duke of Sutherland's zeal for clearing his tenants and, in the second half of the 1800s, many were forcibly removed and emigrated to Nova Scotia and Australia.

There is a car park at the east end of Scourie Beach, signed from the main road. On the right is a wildlife hide, well worth a visit. You could see red- and black-throated divers here, whilst the very patient and quiet might be rewarded by a sighting of an otter. If not, then the sands and aqua-blue water are attraction enough.

Follow the road across the back of the beach towards the cemetery. Keep to the right around the wall and soon go through a gate to reach a bench in a beautiful position with a great view. Look for an indistinct path which runs around the back of the cemetery and then skirts the coast just above an old line of wooden fenceposts. Handa Island can be seen over to the right – it is a stunning bird reserve which is a must-visit on any trip to this area (see p30). Drop downhill to go through another gate and then across the back of a pebbly bay.

After passing through a third gate, keep

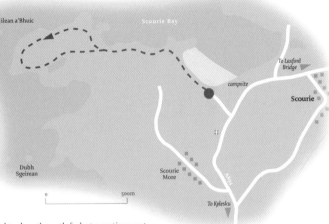

ilean a'Bhuic

Scourie Bay

To Laxford
Bridge

campsite

Scourie

Dubh
Sgeirean

Scourie
More

A894

To Kylesku

0   500m

ght when the path forks to continue out
nto the headland, Rubha Shios. Near the
arthest point, there are a number of cairns
hich mark particularly good viewpoints.
he small island just out to sea is Eilean
Bhuic, whilst along the coast to the left
he massive sea stack of the Old Man of

Stoer can be seen, outlined against the sky.
In very clear conditions, you might even
pick out the Western Isles. Unless intent
on a much longer and tougher walk, it is
best to return by the same route.

Looking across Scourie Bay **29**

Handa Island

Distance 6.5km **Time** 2-3 hours on Handa **Terrain** well-signed footpath, usually dry underfoot, almost level, passes high clifftops **Map** OS Explorer 445 **Access** ferry runs regularly from Tarbet from April to late September Mon-Sat; last ferry to the island 2pm, final ferry back 4:30pm

Take the tiny ferry to Handa Island and experience the magical atmosphere of this nature reserve, home to a large colony of seabirds including puffins and great skuas. Although the best time to see the birds is during early summer, the walk includes sandy beaches, high cliffs and an impressive sea stack, making a superb day out at any time in the season.

To reach Tarbet, take the signed minor road off the A894 between Scourie and Laxford Bridge. A small pier and a few houses – including a great seafood restaurant and café – make up the small, sheltered settlement. The large parking area gives an indication of the popularity of Handa, but even this is sometimes full at the height of summer. The cost of the ride includes a donation to the Scottish Wildlife Trust (SWT) which manages the reserve. The tiny speedboat makes short work of the crossing to the island, landing on a perfect sandy beach. On a hot day, it's tempting to stay here, but each ferry group is ushered to a nearby hut by an SWT volunteer, where a short introduction to the island is given. The stone shelter also has further information about the birds and wildlife.

From here, the well-made path leads northwest to the interior of the island. Pass through a gate to soon find the remains of the main village. The island sustained a population of around 60 until the potato famine caused most of the population to emigrate to Nova Scotia. As well as being farmers, the islanders were skilled climbers, similar to the better known St Kildans, and they, likewise, harvested eggs and birds from the high cliffs.

The ferry landing on Handa Island

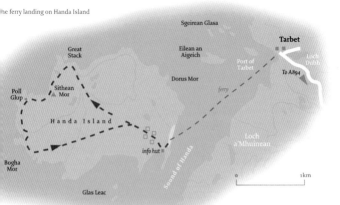

Bear right at the fork, following the sign the Great Stack, and cross an area of en moorland where you may come der fire from Arctic skuas and their ger cousin, the great skua – the Hercules mber of seabirds. Locally known as nxies, the birds are not shy when it mes to defending their territory. During the breeding season, the noise comes ever louder as the cliff edge is pproached. Up to 200,000 birds nest on nda's cliffs every year, a noisy and metimes quarrelsome jumble of illemots, razorbills, kittiwakes – and ffins, after which the bay below the cliffs re is named.

Turn left at the cliff edge and follow the th to a deep geo, or inlet, carved in the m-high cliffs. In the centre of the inlet is e famous Great Stack, its east face seen ead. The Great Stack has remained the eferred nesting place for everyone's favourite seabird, the puffin. Until recently, Handa was inhabited by rats, which raid the nests of puffins; although the rats have now been eradicated, the puffins still favour nesting on the stack. Take the path up to the back of the inlet. It cuts inland from here, but to get better views of the stack you can detour a little way downhill to the right, steering clear of the cliff edge.

The path now crosses to the west side of the island to reach Poll Glup, a great blowhole formed when the roof of a sea cave collapsed. The cliffs steadily decline as the path continues, but there are great views of the mountains of Assynt ahead, as well as the chance to spot dolphins or Minke whales out at sea. Accompany the path from the pebble beach back to the village ruins and, from here, turn right to retrace the outward route past the shelter to await the return ferry at the beach.

Beaches of Oldshoremore Bay

Distance 8km Time 3 hours 30
Terrain rough coastal walking with some
pathless sections and a scramble near the
start; good navigational skills needed;
minor road to return Map OS Explorer 446
Access schoolbus (169) from Durness and
daily bus (806) from Lairg to Kinlochbervie,
3.5km away

This fairly tough coastal walk links some
of the most beautiful and isolated sandy
beaches in Scotland. The inland return by
minor roads passes through tiny crofting
communities. On a fine day, some may
prefer to be left to enjoy the sand and
waves at Oldshoremore.

Oldshoremore is a small community,
part of a crofting estate now owned by the
conservation charity, the John Muir Trust.
In the settlements this walk passes, there
are about 100 permanent residents,
although the numbers swell in the
summer months. To reach the car park for
this walk, follow the signs for
Oldshoremore Bay, taking a left turn off
Blairmore and Sheigra road to descend
steeply towards the shore.

From the car park, go through the gate
next to the toilets and climb to the top of
the dunes. After another gate, steps lead
down onto the superb beach. The fine
white sand is a mixture of ground-up shell
and the local sandstone; behind the beach
it has built up to form a small dune system
and area of machair, which is renowned for
its display of rare flowers in the spring.
Cross to the very far end of the bay – at
high tide there is only a narrow strip of
sand here. Look for a band of red rock,
where a short rough scramble is needed to
reach a faint path on the turf above.
Aim for a stile and, once this is crossed

ead diagonally left uphill rather than
ollowing the clearer flat path also to the
ft. The path is only faint as it climbs a
rassy gully and then bears west, cutting
cross the small headland towards Polin
ay. On reaching a fence, stay on the
oastal side and accompany it around a
orner with a good view of the beach
head. Carefully step over the fence where
here is wood on the top, and follow the
iff path until a point where you can
escend easily to the beach at Polin.

After crossing the pristine sands here,
ook out for the path which starts at a
orner fencepost; it quickly becomes more
istinct as its climbs steeply. Cross a stile
ear the top and then keep right on a small
ath, staying close to the fence. This leads
ver lumpy ground to Port Chaligaig where
small pier provides evidence of a once
important fishing port.

At the bottom, turn right onto the road
nd then very soon left through a gate for
steep uphill climb on the path. Once the

gradient eases off a bit, keep climbing,
remaining fairly close to the sea but safely
back from the cliff edge; there are some
faint paths. Look out for the impressive
sea stacks, standing proud on a wave-cut
platform. After a rusty fencepost, the path
improves and crosses a flat area of
clifftop. Soon, where a stone wall comes
into view, aim for the seaward end and
cross the stile to enjoy the first view of
the sands at Sheigra.

The path follows a wide ledge part way
down the cliff to eventually reach the basic
camping area at Sheigra. Go through the
campsite to head inland on a track, passing
the cemetery along the way. Turn right to
follow the minor road as it passes the
houses dotted amongst the small fields
and open grazing land. Ignore the turnings
to Port Chaligaig and Polin, finally turning
right in Oldshoremore to take the road
down to the beach.

Sandwood Bay

Distance 13km **Time** 4 hours **Terrain** fairly
level track with two (usually easy) water
crossings; The route crosses crofting land
used for livestock grazing and dogs
should be kept under strict control
Map OS Explorer 446 **Access** schoolbus
(169) from Durness and daily bus (806)
from Lairg to Kinlochbervie, 5.4km away

One of the most iconic and photographed
sandy beaches in Britain, **Sandwood Bay**
deserves the accolades. Feeling the full
force of the Atlantic breakers, this massive
beach is wild and vast enough to feel truly
remote – despite its popularity on a busy
summer's day.

NB: The walk to the beach is longer than
many expect; those with very young children or
who just want a quick beach fix may prefer
Oldshoremore Bay just down the road.

Sandwood Bay has taken on an almost
mythical status amongst walkers, with
some people making annual pilgrimages to
a place routinely dubbed 'Britain's most
beautiful beach'. Although the car park and

track can be busy on sunny summer days,
the wild setting and the size of the bay
itself mean you can always find your own
isolated spot. The walk starts from the car
park at Blairmore, reached by taking the
B801 to Kinlochbervie and continuing past
Oldshoremore towards the end of the road
From the car park, cross the road and go
through a gate onto a wide track.

As the track undulates over the open
countryside, it leaves behind the scattered
white houses of the crofting communities
and crosses often bleak heather moorland
The estate is owned by conservation
charity, the John Muir Trust, which bough
it in 1993. Before then, it was possible to
drive along the track towards the beach.
The JMT aims to preserve the rich natural
habitats and wild beauty which is a major
draw for visitors, whilst also supporting
the local community and enabling croftin
to thrive. To date, the strategy seems to be
working with a reasonably harmonious
relationship between landlord and tenant
which, given the turbulent history of such

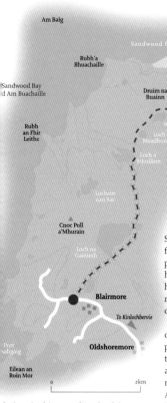

on stepping stones – straightforward except in the wettest weather.

Soon the track narrows and, after a gentle climb, the wild line of cliffs which lead from Sandwood to Cape Wrath come into view in the distance. Two wooden gateposts mark the final section of path and a first view of Sandwood Loch, a large expanse of freshwater set back from the coast and popular with fishermen. The ruin of a house over to the right was said to be haunted by the ghost of a shipwrecked mariner who used to tap on the windows on stormy nights.

The final stage through the maram grass of the dune system is a delight; keep to the path to avoid erosion. Sandwood Loch has the appearance of a lagoon on the right and, once the sands themselves are reached, the great guardian sea stack of Am Buachaille, 'The Herdsman', comes into view at the far south end of the bay. The size of the beach can only be appreciated by walking across it; the best view of the whole expanse is to be had from the north end where it is possible to ascend a little to take in the extent of the sands and the ocean breakers. Most are just content to find a spot near the dunes and watch for dolphins and the occasional mermaid. Return the same way.

...lations in this part of Scotland, is an ...chievement in itself.

Loch Aisir is soon passed and the track ...uns close to a second body of water, Loch ...a Gainimh. After leaving this loch, look ...ut for a path on the left which cuts out a ...orner of the track; if you miss it, stay on ...he track and turn sharp left; the routes ...oon merge. The track now descends to ...och a' Mhuilinn, crossing its feeder burn

Kyle of Durness

Distance **9 km** Time **3-5 hours**
Terrain **rough coastal path with some
pathless sections, short section of road,
path through fields** Map **OS Explorer 446**
Access **bus (806) from Durness to
Balnakeil Craft Village, 500m from start;
can also start from Durness and follow the
road to Balnakeil for 1.5km**

**This beautiful but challenging walk hugs
the coastline with views over the water
towards the Parph, an empty wilderness
extending to Cape Wrath, and the chance
to visit unspoilt sandy beaches.**

Start from Balnakeil car park between
the ruin of Durness Old Church and the
large grey Balnakeil House; do not
continue to the golf course as parking is
for golfers only. Walk along the road
towards the golf course, with good views
over the sandy beach and Faraid Head
beyond. Ignore the stile on the right and

go through the golf course entrance.
Instead of aiming for the clubhouse, bear
slightly right to accompany a grassy path
marked at the start with white pebbles.
The golf club prides itself on being the
most northwesterly on the British
mainland; the final tee involves a daring
leap over the sea, so there's no wonder the
seals are wearing helmets! As you pass the
course, keep an eye out for golfers and try
not to disturb their game.

Keep right at the junction after a bench
to take a narrower path near the cliff edge.
Eventually, when you reach a fence, walk
left up to a gate, passing through this to
continue on a faint path which hugs the
cliffs. Once round the headland, the path
bears south, with great views over the
water to the massive cliffs; those at Clo
Mor, east of Cape Wrath, are the highest on
mainland Britain. After a pleasant section
on springy turf, pass a beach almost cut of

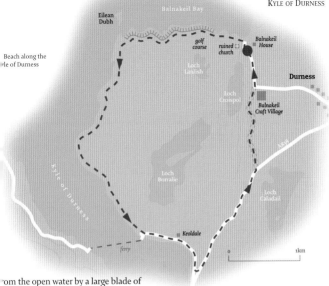

Beach along the
~le of Durness

from the open water by a large blade of
ock. The path travels behind the beach in
he dunes, crossing a stile before coming
o another beach. Here you can choose
etween the dune path or the sands,
lthough it is a bit of a scramble up soft
and to regain the path at the far end.

Keep walking south along the dunes and
hen the clifftop alongside the narrowest
ection of the Kyle. Here, the Cape Wrath
erry can often be seen taking passengers
o the white house on the far shore; a
ninibus ferries them to the Cape itself, a
distance of almost 18km. Soon, the ferry
erminal on the near shore can be seen
head. Descend to it and go through the
ate onto the minor road, following this to
he left until it reaches the main A838.
urn left here and, taking care on the

grassy verge, climb back towards Durness.

Keep an eye out for a signed path for
Balnakeil on the left. Go through the gate
here and follow the footpath along the
field edge. Keep close to the stone wall and
go through another two gates before
passing the Old Manse and taking the
track which skirts along the edge of the
Balnakeil Craft Village.

Although the old RAF buildings are
incongruous to look at, they have become
home to a thriving community of artists
and other small businesses – and this is a
good place to while away an interesting
hour or so and have a bite to eat at the
bookshop. When you meet the road, turn
left and follow it downhill to return to the
car park at the start.

Faraid Head

Distance **6.5km** Time **2 hours**
Terrain **sandy beach, track, path through dunes is indistinct in places; short steep sections but generally easygoing**
Map **OS Explorer 446** Access **bus (806) from Durness to Balnakeil Craft Village, 500m away; can also start from Durness and follow the road to Balnakeil for 1.5km**

Two fabulous sandy beaches backed by an extensive dune system provide the perfect approach to Faraid Head. Look over to the cliffs stretching away towards Cape Wrath and watch out for seabirds and seals on the return.

There is a parking area next to Durness Old Church near Balnakeil, just west of Durness. Opposite is the grey hulk of Balnakeil House, the ancestral seat of the Clan Mackay. It dates back to 1744 but sits on the site of a much more ancient monastery said to have been founded by St Maelrubha in 720. Head down towards the beach, passing through a small gate near the house.

Walk along the sands to the far end. Any tyre tracks here give a clue to what is possibly one of the most beautiful and hair-raising commutes to work. The northern tip of Faraid Head was originally home to a radar station and, although that technology is now obsolete, is still used b

he Ministry of Defence as
 base for the live shelling
xercises regularly inflicted
n Cape Wrath – miraculously,
he large seabird population
ontinues to thrive under this
ombardment. Whilst the sand on
ne beach here is stable, further on
he shifting sands continuously
hange the route of the track, adding
pice to the drive, and there is the
dded obstacle of grazing cows which
often congregate on the warm sands
o top up their tans.

At the far end of the beach, follow
he road across springy turf, well-
rowsed by rabbits and livestock. Go
hrough a gate and, just before the road
ives into the dunes, there are great views
f the larger second beach. The road twists
nd turns to eventually reach an area
vhere the tarmac is usually buried under
he sand. Bear left across this towards a
valled enclosure to soon pick up the road
gain. As it rises towards the MoD base, it
s possible to use small paths to detour out
onto the first, smaller headland on the left.

On reaching the MoD fence, turn right
nd follow it towards the cliffs. Just before
he cliff edge, a cairn is visible on the right
- this is an excellent viewpoint over the
vhole peninsula. Continue along the cliffs,
xeeping eyes peeled for a spectacular trio
of jagged rocks out in the water. In the
pring, this is a good place to spot puffins
nd other nesting seabirds.

Soon after a slight descent, a path bears
right across the peninsula. Although this is
indistinct and joined by many small sheep
and rabbit tracks, keep aiming in the same
direction through the dunes and you
should emerge at the large sandy area
crossed earlier. From here, return to the
road and follow it back to Balnakeil beach
and the start of the walk.

◀ Cows at Balnakeil Bay

Smoo Cave

Distance **7 km** Time **2 hours – allow extra time for exploring the cave** Terrain **long flight of steps down to the cave; inland section is on gravel tracks with a short pavement section** Map **OS Explorer 446** Access **buses (806, 169) from Durness; Tim Dearman Coaches runs daily summer service from Inverness to Smoo Cave**

Just east of Durness lies the massive gaping mouth of Smoo Cave, the largest sea cave in Britain. Explore the cavern and then head inland to experience the total contrast between the complex coastline and the empty moors behind it.

Smoo Cave car park is just past the youth hostel on the A838 east of Durness; there are toilets and a picnic area. The cave lies at the back of a long inlet or creek, the Geodha Smoo, which would once have been part of the cave itself. A succession of roof collapses have left this 600m inlet in front of the cave entrance, caused by both the sea and the Allt Smoo acting on a weak fault in the limestone. Descend the steps from the car park to reach the gaping entrance to the first chamber, which is over 15m high and 60m long. Beyond is a second chamber, accessible via a wooden walkway, where water from the Allt Smoo falls more than 25m through a sink hole into a deep pool. In stormy weather, high tides can make this a dramatic blowhole, driving great blasts of water out through

he roof. The third chamber s accessible only by boat; here are details of trips at he car park.

Smoo Cave is thought to have been used by humans from more than 6000 years ago right up to the more recent past when it was made use of by smugglers. Today, it s a busy attraction, sometimes playing host to a variety of special events, including a visit by the BBC Scottish Symphony Orchestra in 2007 which culminated in a concert in the cave.

After emerging back into daylight, take the sloping path on the other side of the inlet, doubling back near the top to aim inland. Just before the road, a detour to the right allows a good view of the sink hole where the Allt Smoo disappears down a vertical shaft. Return to the main path to reach the road. Cross and turn left, keeping to the pavement as you climb. After passing a track on the right, look out for a new house and a track signed for Bhlar Duibhe. Pass the house and go through the gate to accompany this track over heather moorland.

The interior landscape of this area is now revealed, an apparently endless expanse of moorland and hills interspersed with lochans. At first glance, it can appear bleak, and certainly feels that way if out in a horizontal hailstorm; however, on a clear day it is possible to appreciate its harsh beauty and remoteness.

After rising gently for some distance, you come to a junction with the track leading to the bealach. Turn right and follow the Allt Smoo downstream. After a short while, cross this on stepping stones and join the track from Loch Meadaidh, which can be seen in the distance. Take this to the right, continuing on the surfaced road after the gate. At the main road, turn right to follow the pavement past the community hall and back to the Smoo Cave car park.

◀ Gaping entrance to Smoo Cave

Ceannabeinne and the Durness Riots

Distance **1km** Time **45 minutes**
Terrain **waymarked route through open croftland with some high bracken in summer** Map **OS Explorer 446**
Access **nearest bus stop is at Smoo Cave, 2.6km away**

Step back 170 years in time when this peaceful spot was buzzing with the sound of a riotous mob, prepared to risk everything to fight against eviction. This short walk explores the township of Ceannabeinne where many of the rioters lived, bringing to life a brutal episode in Highland history.

From Durness, take the A838 east towards Tongue for 5km, looking for an unobtrusive layby with an information board on the left-hand side. This is the start of a marked heritage trail which wanders through the remains of the settlement overlooking the sandy bay of Tràigh Allt Chailgeag.

This place was once home to a settled community of about 50 people, or 10 families, living as tenants to the Duke of Sutherland and growing crops, fishing and keeping some livestock. The cottage a little distance away on the far side of the road was the local school and is the only building from the 1800s to have survived in the immediate area.

By 1841, the process of clearing the land to make way for profitable sheep had been well established in other parts of Sutherland and the Highlands. Other changes, including the growth of industrial jobs in the cities, easier opportunities to travel and the availability of paid jobs from big sheep farms or the fishing industry in Caithness, were also fuelling the erosion of the traditional township way of life.

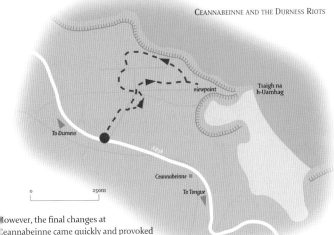

viewpoint

Traigh na h-Uamhag

To Durness

Ceannabeinne

To Tongue

0   250m

However, the final changes at Ceannabeinne came quickly and provoked a furious response. In September, the Duke's tacksman, John Anderson, sent a sheriff officer with an eviction notice to the village on a day when the men were away cutting grass. According to local reports, the women held the officer's hand to the fire until the notice was burnt through. Two more attempts at eviction also met resistance before the sheriff returned with 4 police officers on a Sunday, intent on enforcing the eviction notices. Word had already got out, and approximately 50 local men attacked the sheriff's party as they gathered at a local inn and they were driven from the area in what became known as the Durness Riots.

The evictions were eventually enforced by threat of army intervention, and the township at Ceannabeinne fell silent when the last residents left in 1842. However, the riots gave publicity to the tenants' plight and played a part in the build-up of public sympathy which led to the eventual passing of the Crofters Act in 1886, giving tenants security on their crofts.

Although there is no clear path, the walk is easy to follow if you look out for the arrow posts pointing the way to each of the information boards that tell the full story. Start by aiming downhill before passing through a gap in the stone wall on the right. From the next information board, bear sharply left to cross a wooden bridge. The route heads towards the coast and then follows marker posts to the left and another board. Here, you can climb the small hillock to the right to look across the fabulous sandy beach and over the water to the forbidding cliffs of Whiten Head. After going through a gap in a stone wall, you'll reach the remains of a row of cottages. From here, bear left to rejoin the outward route, crossing back over the bridge and following the wall to the right to return through the gap to the layby.

◀ Ruins at Ceannabeinne

Durness

Whiten
Head

Strathy
Point

Loch Eriboll

①

② Bettyhill

Tongue

Loch Hope

Loch
Loyal

③

④

This is the biggest but emptiest part of the Far North. The deeply indented northern coastline has fine beaches and villages such as Tongue and Bettyhill. Stretching inland between the vast bogs are long, fertile straths which may appear more welcoming but are almost completely devoid of settlement. It was here, particularly in Strathnaver, that some of the most notoriously ruthless episodes in the Highland Clearances were played out; a visit to the Strathnaver Museum at Bettyhill is recommended.

Further south is Lairg; it is really just a large village at a junction of roads, but is an important centre for miles around. The austere Loch Shin stretches away from here, but in other directions the landscape becomes softer and more intimate. The Falls of Shin may not be particularly high, but the great power of the water is usually very impressive; this has become famous as a place to watch for leaping salmon. This area has plenty of easier waymarked forest walks and contrasts strikingly with the wilderness to the north.

Lairg

⑤

⑥

Brora

⑦

Golspie

Bonarbridge

Dornoch

Strathnaver after the rains ▶

Dornoch
Firth

Central Sutherland

Talmine Pier and Port Vasgo

Distance 10km Time 3 hours 30
Terrain **rough, pathless section along the
coast, very quiet minor road; the path and
track over the moors are often muddy**
Map OS Explorer 447 Access **schoolbus
(169) from Durness and (172) from
Bettyhill to Talmine**

**This excellent, varied trek takes in most
aspects of the wild Sutherland coastline.
The rough terrain is rewarded by a remote
sandy bay and a moorland crossing with a
real wilderness feel.**

Talmine is visited by few, but is well
worth the short detour along a minor road
from the west side of the Kyle of Tongue.
There is a small parking area near the pier
at the far end of the beach, where you can
view the Rabbit Islands with their
tantalising sandy beaches out of reach of
landlubbers. Follow the grassy track signed
for Port Vasgo, which soon becomes a
vague coastal path. Keep left where the
path forks; Eilean nan Ron, 'The Island of
the Seals', comes into view, either with or
without seals basking on the rocks –
depending on the time of year. After a
while, the path peters out completely and
the ground becomes alternately boggy and
rocky. Keep safely back from the steep
slopes dropping into the water, and
eventually bear left over broken ground to
reach an old stone-built ramp that leads
down to the deep bay at Port Vasgo.

The waters here have seen their fair share
of action, being strategically placed at the
far north of Britain. After the defeat of
Bonnie Prince Charlie at the Battle of
Culloden in 1746, a ship carrying gold from
the French King Louis XV was shipwrecked
here as it tried to bring supplies to the
Young Pretender and his followers, who
were hiding in the Scottish islands. The
ship had been chased by a naval frigate

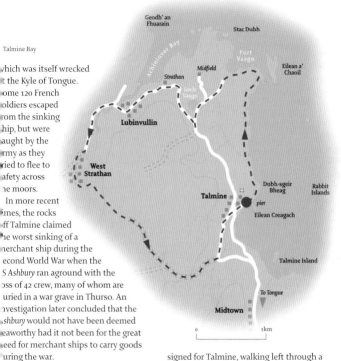

Talmine Bay

which was itself wrecked
at the Kyle of Tongue.
Some 120 French
soldiers escaped
from the sinking
ship, but were
caught by the
army as they
tried to flee to
safety across
the moors.

In more recent
times, the rocks
off Talmine claimed
the worst sinking of a
merchant ship during the
Second World War when the
SS Ashbury ran aground with the
loss of 42 crew, many of whom are
buried in a war grave in Thurso. An
investigation later concluded that the
Ashbury would not have been deemed
seaworthy had it not been for the great
need for merchant ships to carry goods
during the war.

At Port Vasgo, head left to follow the
minor road uphill and past some modern
houses. Ignore the turning for Midfield,
passing Loch Vasgo to reach a T-junction.
Turn right here, passing the houses at
Strathan. The lovely sandy beach at
Achininver can be reached by a short,
signed detour to the right.

Continuing along the road, turn left
towards West Strathan after crossing the
burn. At the end of the road, take the path

signed for Talmine, walking left through a
gate. Keep the burn on your right as you
aim for a large footbridge over the Strath
Melness Burn. After crossing this, the path
rises diagonally right across the moor. Pass
a stone seat and carry on along the
improving track as it makes the moorland
crossing, with excellent views towards Ben
Loyal, known as the 'Queen of Scottish
Mountains'. At length, the track descends
to the road. Turn left and finally fork right
at the junction to return to Talmine Pier.

Invernaver Broch and Torrisdale Beach

Distance 6.5km **Time** 2 hours 30
Terrain rough walking with some steep
and pathless sections as well as dunes and
a sandy beach; navigation skills needed
Map OS Explorer 448 **Access** nearest bus
stop is at Bettyhill, 500m away

This tougher walk has typical north coast
scenery, with good views over a wide beach
as well as inland up the strath. It visits a
strategically positioned iron age broch
before crossing moorland to descend to the
dramatic dunes and wide beach of
Torrisdale Bay. The whole area covered by
the walk is a nature reserve designated as a
Site of Special Scientific Interest.

The walk starts from the road end at
Invernaver, just north of the A836 to
Bettyhill. There is only very limited
parking here, and care should be taken
not to block any house or field entrances.
If there is insufficient space, it is better
to park in the layby just over the bridge

towards Bettyhill on the main road.

From the loop section of road, head
towards the coast by going through the
small metal gate next to the last house. Bear
left over the field and down to the shore.
A faint track follows a line of telegraph poles
beneath the high hill on the left, crossing a
small burn on stepping stones.

Just before the way ahead is obstructed
by a large area of raised beach and dunes,
take a path to the left which clambers up a
cleft in the hillside, still keeping to the
telegraph poles. A narrow path on the left
side of the burn takes you uphill until you
are opposite a distinctive lump on the
other side of the water. Although, from
this angle, it looks to be an unimpressive
pile of stones, this is the remains of a large
iron age broch and it is well worth crossing
the burn to visit it.

The easiest way is to walk up to the
small shoulder between the broch and the
rest of the hill and then turn right to

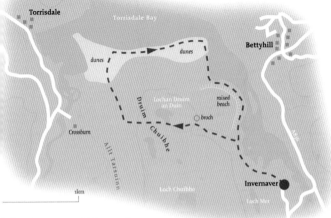

climb to the entrance which cannot be seen from below. Once on top of the thick wall, it is clear why this location was chosen. The broch is a fantastic vantage point with long sightlines inland along the River Naver and, more importantly, out to sea with the ability to spot approaching vessels in time to warn of a possible attack. Structures such as this one would have been used by iron age settlers to shelter, together with their animals, when Norwegian and other raiders attacked.

After visiting the broch, continue upstream to pick up a faint path. The ground levels off and there are a number of indistinct trods running through the undergrowth of heather, juniper and crowberry; keep following the line of the telegraph poles. The path passes the side of Lochan Druim an Duin, but ignore the fisherman's path around the lochan – instead dropping downhill on a lower stretch of ground where the telegraph

poles run. The path improves as the route descends to the large flat area at sea level, with the small settlement of Torrisdale visible across the bay.

At the bottom of the slope, aim diagonally to the right to meet a wider path and turn right to accompany this through bracken and then across the dunes, continuing more or less straight ahead until you emerge onto the wide sands. Bear right to cross the sands of Torrisdale Bay towards Bettyhill and, at the far end, go right to shadow the River Naver upstream and eventually rejoin the outward route. If the tide is high, you may need to climb up onto the raised beach and cross this rather than staying close to the riverside. This area is a warren of chambered cairns, cists and other neolithic remains, although not much is visible to the untrained eye. Continue south to return to Invernaver.

Rosal Clearance Village

Distance **4km** Time **1 hour 30**
Terrain **clear, waymarked paths, forestry track; the undulating route through the village is on grassy paths which can be wet underfoot** Map **OS Explorer 448**
Access **no public transport**

Step back in time to discover both the hardships and the close-knit community of crofting life, as recorded by the residents of Rosal. The sad ruins are now inhabited only by munching sheep, as it was here that some of the most notorious episodes of the Highland Clearances took place. The villagers were forced to start afresh on the barren coastline – or to emigrate to Canada, New Zealand or America in search of a better life.

Remote and almost empty today, Strathnaver's fertile land has been settled and farmed for more than 7000 years; this walk explores the remains of the cleared village of Rosal, now a sheep pasture almost surrounded by forestry plantation. To reach it, take the well-signed track off the B871 just east of the junction with the B873 at Syre. If driving from the north, the relative shelter and wide river of the strath provides a strong contrast with the bleak moorland of the coast.

Some way along the track you'll find an information board and car parking area. Starting here, go through the gate and take the track into the forest. Ignore the path on the left immediately after the gate, and continue for almost 1km to a blue marker post beside the track which indicates where a path leads into the trees on the left. Follow this on a winding uphill course to the edge of the forest, bearing right here to reach the gate giving entry to the Rosal township area. Although the tenants were forcibly cleared from the land to make way for sheep, the fenced area is – rather ironically – now used for sheep grazing.

The factor responsible for the evictions

Sheep on the Rosal Trail

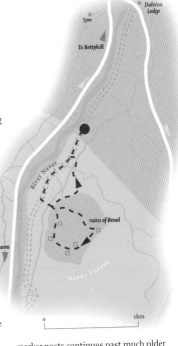

ere was the notorious Patrick Sellar, mployed by the Countess of Sutherland. His grand house can be seen a little further p the strath. By the time of the Rosal learance in 1814, the Industrial Revolution and the growth of the textile industry in Northern England had made sheep farming extremely profitable and this, combined with the Sutherlands' belief that change was in the best interests of tenants who were living at subsistence levels, set the stage for one of the darker episodes of Highland history. In total, more than 15,000 people were cleared from the Sutherland estates, with many evictions carried out with brutal force – in some cases, houses were burnt to the ground. Sellar was himself brought to trial after the torching of a nearby village in which a 92-year-old woman died. Although Sellar was acquitted of culpable homicide, the case helped to push the crofters' plight into the national consciousness.

The route around the scant remains is marked by posts and proceeds in a clockwise direction. The houses were built with only a few courses of stone and then made up with turf and a heather thatch supported by a cruck frame. Only the lower stones remain today but the information boards bring the site to life, many drawing on the writings of one Donald Macleod who recorded memories and stories of his childhood life here.

Climbing uphill, the route between the marker posts continues past much older archaeological remains such as hut circles, souterrains and cairns dating back to the bronze age. On the way back downhill, a short diversion on duckboard shows an example of peat cutting. Many people locally still cut peats to burn in the winter, although cutting and drying is no longer the communal activity it once was. From the duckboard, return to the main path to head through the lower part of the village and back to the start.

Forsinard Dubh Lochan Trail

Distance **1.5km** Time **45 minutes**
Terrain **flagstone trail across a flat bog; although family friendly, it is not suitable for buggies and special care should be taken with small children ; the RSPB does not allow dogs on the walk – there is a forest track nearby where they are welcome** Map **OS Explorer 449** Access **train from Wick, Thurso and Lairg to Forsinard, with connection to Inverness**

Step out onto the watery world of the largest blanket bog in Europe. This short trail across part of an important RSPB reserve is a great chance to explore the amazing habitat and wide-ranging views of the Flow Country.

If anywhere could be said to be in the middle of nowhere then it is Forsinard. Despite having a railway station and hotel (stalking, hawking and fishing are specialities), it is only a tiny hamlet on the A897 surrounded by the seemingly endless peat bogs of the Flow Country. This is a vital habitat for a wide variety of birds, including hen harriers, merlin, greenshank and short-eared owls, and the RSPB own and manage 100 sq km as a nature reserve.

The station building houses an information centre where children can borrow an explorer's backpack and adults can book onto guided walks of the reserve. For the Dubh Lochan Trail, go over the level crossing on the main road and keep

alking south along the road for 200m. ook out for a sign on the right indicating he start of the flagstone path. Take care to tep in the centre of each stone as the dges have a nasty habit of flipping you off nto the bog.

Many come here for the unique irdwatching opportunities, but down at round level there's a whole world of rare arnivorous plants, brightly coloured nosses and, of course, the gloop of the wet eat itself to explore. The Flow Country ame under grave threat during the 1980s ue to land drainage for massive forestry lantations made profitable by tax breaks, nd saving the bogs became a *cause célèbre* f the conservation movement.

A short way onto the trail, the signs of raditional, smaller-scale peat cuttings can e seen in the ridges and depressions on he ground. The peat from this articular spot was shipped

to distilleries all over Scotland and burnt beneath the coppers. Straight ahead, the cone of Ben Griam Beg rises starkly from the flat landscape; its summit is crowned by Scotland's highest hill fort.

Where the path forks, keep left to emerge onto a section of bog still in its natural state. In summer, the small pools swarm with dragonflies. A short detour to the left leads to a rather unique picnic table; get here early and the morning mist can create the impression that the table is floating above the bog. Back on the main trail, follow the flags past a carved wooden seat before the walkway winds between the Dubh Lochan, or 'Dark Pools', and rejoins the outward route.

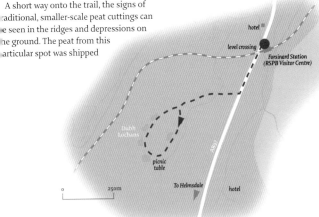

Trail flagstones and Ben Griam Beg

The Ord and Ferry Wood

Distance 5km Time 2 hours
Terrain clear waymarked paths and tracks
with gentle ascents; the Ferry Wood
section is built to all-abilities standards
and is suitable for buggies and some
wheelchairs Map OS Explorer 441
Access buses and train to Lairg

Follow the sheep to the Ferrycroft Visitor
Centre where two waymarked trails can
be combined to give good views over
Loch Shin and Lairg, together with
impressive archaeological remains from
the ancient peoples who once lived here.

Signs and wooden sheep point the way
to the Ferrycroft Visitor Centre to the west
of the River Shin. There is an interesting
display here, as well as a café and wooden
animals that children will befriend. From
the car park, follow the Ferry Wood forest
walks sign, heading past the sports field
on the right and through two gates to
enter the wood. Pass an information board
and picnic table, and keep to the green
waymarkers. Look out for the dragonfly
and large frog at the lochan on the left!

When the path forks, keep right to reach
the shores of Little Loch Shin, with the

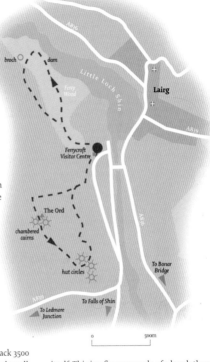

uses of Lairg reflected in water. The path now nges into the mixed odland before reaching a aring with a small grassy und on the right. This is all t remains of Dun Coille, the rt of the Woods', a 10m-high, ble-walled circular tower or ch dating from the iron age. e path curves to the left to run ngside open moorland before entering the forest.

Return to the visitor centre d this time take the path ned for Ord Hill on the far e of the building. A metal te gives access to the open und; keep left to pass near e back of the houses before aring right uphill on a good th. The faint remains of a olithic hut circle are soon ched, one of a range of haeological remains dating back 3500 ars when this area was obviously well pulated and farmed.

At the next junction, turn right and low the marker posts uphill. Carry aight on when the path forks to head wards the mast on top of Ord Hill. On the ht at the summit are the imposing nains of a huge burial cairn, thought to ve served the whole community and to te back more than 5000 years. Bear left to ach the upright stones by the summit

itself. This is a finer example of a broch than the one in the woods, with good views down the length of Loch Shin to Ben Klibreck, one of very few mountains with Munro status in the far north. The marker posts lead you on a diagonal descent in a southeasterly direction at first, passing a depression which may have been either a cooking pit or a steam pit used for washing. Turn right on rejoining the track and retrace your steps to the information centre.

Lairg reflected in Little Loch Shin

Raven's Rock Gorge

Distance 1.5km Time 45 minutes
Terrain good paths with steps and wooden
bridges; take care with children near river
and sides of gorge Map OS Explorer 441
Access no public transport

Voted one of the UK's top ten walks by
the Forestry Commission, Raven's Rock
Gorge (yes, owned and maintained by
the FC) is a magical spot, completely
hidden until you stumble into it. The car
park can be reached by following the
signs from either the A837 or the A839
near Rosehall.

From the car park and picnic area, follow
the red waymarked path as it heads down
into the trees. Where the path forks,
continue straight ahead. A mixed

woodland of spruce, Scots pine, silver fir,
beech and silver birch, the forest supports
a diverse range of wildlife, including the
elusive pine marten – maybe if you come
armed with their favourite jam
sandwiches and wait until sunset you
might strike it lucky. Once down by the
rushing waters of the Allt Mor (which
means 'Big Burn'), turn right and soon
you will encounter a much larger beast,
seen rising up on its hind legs.

The brown bear was in fact one of the
earliest large mammals to become extinct
in Scotland, dying out well before the
Norman conquest. Although there has
been talk of reintroducing some key
species, including wolves and lynx once
habitat can support them, so far only an

The gorge

perimental release of European beavers
Argyll has actually got off the ground, so
eing bears for real in these woods is
obably some way off. Ravens do,
wever, roost in the gorge, allowing
o live up to its name.

The gorge walls become steeper and, as
e path runs alongside the burn, it crosses
sed wooden boardwalks and ascends
light of steps. Eventually, the path
climbs out of the mossy, dark atmosphere
of the ravine and reaches a viewing area
with a seat overlooking a waterfall.

Follow the path to the right to curve back
through the forest above the top of the
gorge, passing through pleasant woodland
and allowing the odd glimpse down to the
bear sculpture below. When you reach a
path junction, turn left to head uphill back
to the car park.

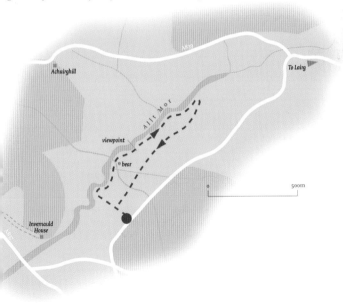

Carbisdale Castle

Distance 4km **Time** 1 hour 30
Terrain good waymarked paths
Map OS Explorer 441 **Access** train from
Lairg or Dingwall and Inverness to
Invershin or Culráin. Add 1.5km to walk
if starting from Invershin

**Explore the estate of the magnificent
Carbisdale Castle which provides amazing
accommodation for youth hostellers. The
grounds are a mixture of forestry and
more open countryside and are popular
with mountain bikers as well as walkers.**

There are two options for the start of this
walk, either the forestry car park near
Culráin accessible along a minor road from
Ardgay or, perhaps more conveniently, the
layby on the A836 at Invershin, opposite
Carbisdale Castle. If starting from Invershin,
cross the footbridge attached to the large
railway bridge over the Kyle of Sutherland.
When the footpath emerges on a road, turn
right and then left up the driveway for
Carbisdale Castle; the Forestry Commission

car park is well signed on the left.

From the car park, take the path marked
with blue posts, keeping an eye out for
mountain bikers as this section is on a
shared route. Very soon, turn right at the
junction and then right again onto the
main driveway to the castle. The castle is
relatively modern, having been built
between 1906 and 1917 by the then
Duchess of Sutherland; however, it packs
powerful punch in its short history.

The Duchess had been married to the 3
Duke of Sutherland, a man of immense
wealth and the owner of nearby Dunrobi
Castle. The Duchess had never been
popular with the in-laws and, following h
death, they contested the will. She was
briefly imprisoned, having destroyed
several vital documents. As part of the
eventual settlement, the Sutherland fami
agreed to fund a new home for the
Duchess on the basis that it must be buil
outside the vast Sutherland estates. The
Duchess duly erected Carbisdale Castle

Carbisdale Castle

ight on the boundary and, as a final snub
o her ex-in laws, the clocktower has three
aces, with the side facing Sutherland left
lank as if to say 'I won't even give you the
ime of day'. The castle was sold to a
Norwegian shipping merchant in the 1930s
nd provided refuge for the Crown Prince
Olav during the Nazi occupation of
Norway. Later, the building was
equeathed to the Scottish Youth Hostel
Association and has been host to
umerous walking groups, weddings and
ackpacker parties. The marble statues and
ong gallery can now be enjoyed while
taying in bunks for bargain prices.

Just before the castle, turn left and then
eft again, following the blue posts uphill.
Cross a bike trail to shortly turn right and
each a viewpoint over the Kyle of
Sutherland. Walk down through the trees,
urning right at a picnic table and then
sharp left to pass a bench and
meet a track. Turn

right here to climb alongside a burn with
pretty waterfalls, continuing straight
ahead to a lochan. Take a left to Montrose
Bridge and stay on the path to reach the
site of the Battle of Carbisdale, fought in
1650 by the Royalist Marquis of Montrose
against the Scottish government of the
time and the radical Covenanting Kirk
Party which controlled it. Bear left up
through the trees to cross a bridge and
then right onto a forest track, keeping
right at the next junction. Just before the
houses, go left onto a path signed for the
castle. This leads past the old walled
garden to the T-junction near the start.
Turn right here to plunge through thick
rhododendrons and return to the car park.

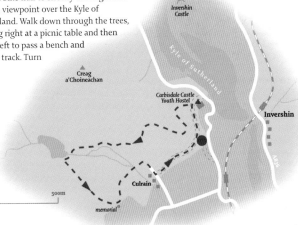

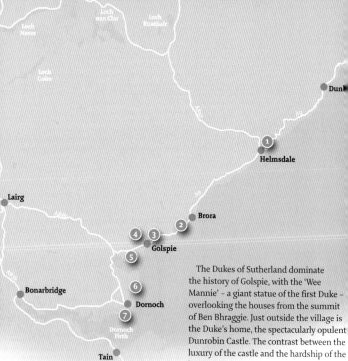

The Dukes of Sutherland dominate the history of Golspie, with the 'Wee Mannie' – a giant statue of the first Duke – overlooking the houses from the summit of Ben Bhraggie. Just outside the village is the Duke's home, the spectacularly opulent Dunrobin Castle. The contrast between the luxury of the castle and the hardship of the lives of the tenants at the time of the Clearances is hard to comprehend.

The next village, Brora, houses a distillery, harbour, sandy beaches and an industrial past. Finally, attractive Helmsdale, now a sleepy place at the foot of Kildonan Strath, became the hub of a gold rush in 1869. After the discovery of a large nugget in the river here, more than 600 adventurers came north to seek their fortune before the issuing of licences to prospectors ceased and the rush ended as suddenly as it had begun.

The eastern coastline is the most populated part of Sutherland. There are still long sandy beaches, but in other ways this region contrasts with the rest of the county, with a string of four substantial settlements by the sea. Southernmost of these is Dornoch, a beautiful Royal Burgh famous for its championship golf links, often included on lists of the best in the world. Heading north is Loch Fleet, a tidal basin and National Nature Reserve renowned for its birdlife.

Helmsdale Harbour ▶

East Sutherland

Helmsdale circuit

Distance 6km **Time** 2 hours
Terrain paths, narrow and slightly
overgrown at times with one steep
stretch; the walk crosses the busy A9
Map OS Explorer 444 **Access** trains and
buses to Helmsdale

**This varied circular explores both the
coastline below and hillside above
Helmsdale, a pretty fishing village with
Viking origins.**

Helmsdale is situated on the A9 north of
Brora. There is a parking area at the west end
of the main street (the A897 road to
Kinbrace), where there are also public toilets.
From here, cross the road and walk down
the street beside the Spar shop, passing
Timespan, an excellent heritage centre
which tells the story of Helmsdale. At the
bottom of the hill, stay on the pavement to
walk alongside the river towards the sea.
Just before the bridge carrying the A9, turn
right onto a footpath that passes under the
bridge to reach the harbour.

Fishing has been an important occupation
since the 15th century, but it was not until
the town was developed as a fishing port in
the early 1800s that the number of boats
expanded to a peak of 204 in 1814. It was at
this time that the huge ice house seen near
the start of the walk was constructed.
A shallow pond behind the structure
provided ice in the winter, although there
are records of ice being imported from
Norway during mild winters. The ice was
kept in the inner chamber and used in the
outer room to pack fish which would then
be sent either by boat to Aberdeen or by rail
to markets in Edinburgh and Glasgow.
Originally there were two ice houses, one
reserved for salmon and one for white fish.
In addition, herring would be salted or
smoked before export.

Follow the harbourside to the left past a

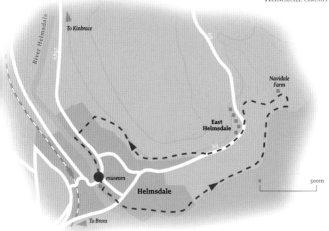

ow of cottages and continue straight
ahead on a lane along the coastline,
passing a derelict building. Just before a
bungalow, turn right to follow the coast
path – with excellent views of the cliffs.
After rounding the headland, the rough
path skirts the back of the pebble-strewn
bay. Cross a small burn and aim for the
ruined house beyond. Here, a path rises
steeply uphill and then turns left onto a
grassy track. At the top of the cliff, just
before a gate, go left to take a narrow path
alongside a fence. When, shortly, this
meets a lane at a white cottage, turn left.
The cemetery on your left is worth a short
detour for its spectacular clifftop setting.
The lane climbs up to join the busy A9,
where you turn left for a short section
along the verge – best to keep on the grass
behind the crash barrier! Just before the
roundabout, cross the A9 to a path on the
far side and follow it left, crossing the

smaller exit road before continuing on the
A9 pavement towards Helmsdale.

Where the pavement ends, it is necessary
to cross again briefly, but look out for a
track heading up between a white cottage
and a taller house on the right-hand side of
the road. This takes you up the hillside
with good views over the town. Just after a
house, turn right up a flight of steps and
continue on the rougher path through
gorse bushes to reach a flagpole. There are
good views up the Strath of Kildonan
before the route descends steeply and
finally reaches the road. Turn right past a
first block of houses and then go left
between the houses to a parking area.
From here, a path leads right and then left
to drop to the river. Bear left to take the
lovely riverside path back to Helmsdale,
before ascending a flight of steps from a
picnic area to return abruptly to the car
park at the start.

Above Helmsdale

63

Brora to Golspie

Distance 11km (one-way) **Time** 3 hours 30
Terrain rough coastal path, can be very
muddy in places through fields
Map OS Explorer 441 **Access** train to return
from Golspie to Brora or to access the
start; there are also buses (N12); check
timetables before setting out

This superb linear walk follows the
coastline between the towns of Brora and
Golspie. The route passes a well-preserved
iron age broch, beaches and Dunrobin
Castle, the 189-room fairytale palace of the
Dukes of Sutherland.

Starting from the train station in the
centre of Brora, turn left (south) along the
main A9 road. Once over the River Brora,
turn left again to follow a lane under the
railway. Descend steps leading to the river
and pass the old ice house to reach the
small harbour. At the far end, take the
ramp up to rejoin the road and keep left to

follow it along the shoreline. Turn left at a
white bungalow to reach the beach and a
footpath sign for Golspie.

At first, the route follows a track to the
left of some portacabins; thereafter, you
can choose either a path in the dunes
beside the fence or to take to the sands.
After 2km, the dune path drops down to
the beach where the Sputie Burn cascades
onto the shore. After crossing the water,
you can once more either regain the dunes
or continue on the beach. Eventually,
the two routes merge on the sand
near a cave. Soon after this, go
through a kissing gate and
carry on along a path until
you see the remains of
Carn Liath Broch ahead.

This iron age defensive
structure is well worth
the short detour. The
track takes you alongside

Golspie
Tower

Golspie

Dunrobin Castle seen from the shore

e fence where you then turn right to
xplore the 2000-year-old broch, probably
sed to shelter families and animals
uring raids by the Norwegians. The
ouble-walled structure and the bottom
art of a staircase between the walls can
early be seen.

Return to the foreshore and continue on
pringy turf, sometimes wet underfoot.
fter crossing two small burns, a gate leads
ou into woodland. Keep straight ahead at
junction and pass some houses
elonging to the Sutherland Estate. Soon
he Disneyesque turrets of Dunrobin
astle come into view. The castle, the
ncestral home of the Earls and Dukes
f Sutherland, is well worth a visit
o gawp at the amazing display
f wealth. Even more jaw-
ropping is the museum in
he grounds containing
poils from their

African safaris and other hunting trips,
which include giraffes, leopards and
elephants. Some parts of the castle date
back to 1225, but most of the structure
seen today was remodelled in 1845 by
Charles Barry, who was also the architect
responsible for the Houses of Parliament
and very much in fashion at the time.
If you have also visited Badbea in
Caithness (see p94) then it is hard to
reconcile the splendour here with the
appalling life of some of the Sutherlands'
tenants during the same period.

Keep following the track past the castle

and cross a grassy
field to a gate at a
cottage. Another gate gives
access to the Golspie Burn which
is crossed on a footbridge adjacent to a
beautiful house. A street of picturesque
Sutherland estate houses and offices leads
up to the main road. If catching a train, the
station is at the far (southern) end of
Golspie, so turn left along the main road
and follow it through the centre.

65

Big Burn

Distance 2.5km **Time** 1 hour
Terrain good woodland paths, steps and
steep slopes in places **Map** OS Explorer 441
Access Golspie train station is 1.5km away
at the opposite end of the village; also
regular bus services

Explore the secrets of this wee hidden
glen, crossing and recrossing the river as
you pass through Big Burn gorge. There is
a fine waterfall before the walk climbs out
of the gorge and returns via a mill pond.
Plenty of interest for both children and
wildlife enthusiasts on this short and
popular route.

At the northern end of Golspie, between

the Golspie Inn and Sutherland Stonework
and the bridge, a track on the west side of
the road gives access to a car park signed
for Big Burn. Begin on the clear path which
leads upstream. Golspie Mill can be seen
on the opposite bank, one of very few
traditional watermills still making flour.
Cross the burn on a stone footbridge and
pass under the towering arch of the railway
viaduct. The path branches off to the left to
a picnic area but this walk continues ahead.

When the path forks, keep to the bottom
of the glen, following the yellow
waymarkers through the lush vegetation.
Soon, the rocky entrance to Big Burn gorge
is reached. Footbridges cross the burn

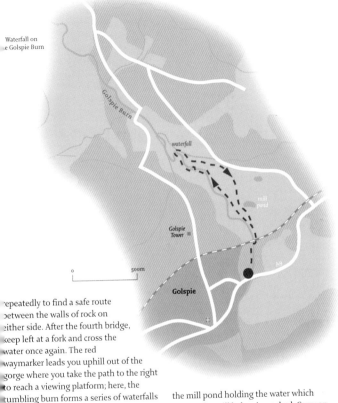

Waterfall on
~e Golspie Burn

Golspie Burn

waterfall

mill
pond

Golspie
Tower

0   500m

A9

Golspie

~epeatedly to find a safe route
~etween the walls of rock on
~ither side. After the fourth bridge,
~eep left at a fork and cross the
water once again. The red
waymarker leads you uphill out of the
gorge where you take the path to the right
~o reach a viewing platform; here, the
~umbling burn forms a series of waterfalls
~n a dramatic scene that children will love.
After this detour, return to the main path
and, this time, climb the steps.

Cross the bridge above the waterfalls and
turn right at the next two junctions to
continue, now high above the gorge,
passing a small car park on the left. Soon

the mill pond holding the water which
powers the mill below is reached. Carry on
ahead or to the left to follow the loop
around the water before taking the path on
the right which drops back down to the Big
Burn. Once the outward path is met, turn
left along the glen and pass back under the
railway line to return to the start.

Ben Bhraggie

Distance 9km Time 4 hours
Terrain waymarked paths and forest
tracks, some steep sections; care should
be taken to look out for mountain bikes
crossing the route Map OS Explorer 441
Access bus and train services to Golspie

Climb steeply to reach the Wee Mannie,
the massive Sutherland monument which
overlooks many miles of the eastern
coastline. From the summit on a clear day,
a keen eye may pick out the distant west
coast as well as the mountains of the
north. Extra excitement is added by the
tortuous mountain bike routes and
obstacles passed on the way up.

The ascent of Ben Bhraggie starts from
the centre of Golspie. There is a large car
park where Fountain Road branches off the
main street. From here, walk up Fountain
Road away from the town, passing under
the railway and a second car park for the
Highland Wildcat Trails. These mountain
bike routes were created in 2006 and
provide some of the most varied and

challenging rides in Scotland. If you've
ever fancied balancing a bike across a
slippery log or hurtling down a steep,
water-filled track with obstacles at every
turn, this is your place. The information
accompanying the trails highlights the
nearby minor injuries unit, so it goes
without saying that adrenalin and padding
are needed in equal quantities.

The comparatively sedate walking option
heads up the road, passing a grand house
and Rhives Farm steading. When the track
forks, keep left and carry on uphill past a
water tank. Once amongst the trees, the
track curves right. Soon after, take a signed
path left which leads more steeply uphill,
and then follow a signed path right past
open ground with pylons, crossing a track

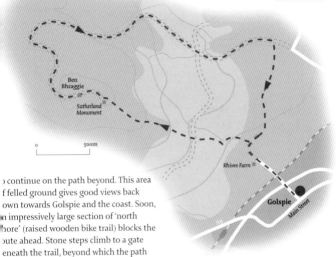

Ben
Bhraggie

Sutherland
Monument

0   500m

Rhives Farm

Golspie

Main Street

continue on the path beyond. This area
f felled ground gives good views back
own towards Golspie and the coast. Soon,
n impressively large section of 'north
hore' (raised wooden bike trail) blocks the
oute ahead. Stone steps climb to a gate
eneath the trail, beyond which the path
imbs up to the Sutherland Monument.
The 30m-high statue dominates the
oastline for miles around. Standing at the
ase, you can hardly see the statue because
f the sheer bulk of the enormous plinth.
he plaque claims that it was erected in
837 by 'a mourning and grateful tenantry'
o 'a judicious, kind and liberal landlord'.
he monument commemorates George
Granville Leveson-Gower who also went
nder the titles of Baron Gower of
tittenham, Viscount Trentham, Earl
ower and the 2nd Marquis of Stafford as
vell as the 1st Duke of Sutherland. It was
n his role as landowner that the Duke of
utherland became infamous for his part
n the forced Clearances of tenants to make
vay for profitable sheep in the early 19th
entury. After his death in 1833,
ubscriptions were raised from the

remaining tenantry to pay for the statue
which has remained controversial ever
since. In the 1970s, talk was rife of a plot to
blow it up, but more recently calls have
been made for it to be relocated to
Dunrobin Castle.

Follow the clear track inland across
heather moorland. Eventually it curves
right and aims downhill. Pass Larson's Well
which provided water for the men and
horses based at a camp here during the
construction of the monument. Once
amongst the trees, the path reaches a
crossroads; turn right along the forestry
track and then keep left when the route
forks. When you come to the point where
you crossed this track on the way up, turn
left to follow the path back down to a
track; turn right here to head down past
Rhives Farm and back to Golspie.

Loch Fleet National Nature Reserve

Distance **7.5km** Time **2 hours**
Terrain **waymarked path, forest tracks
with optional rough shoreline**
Map **OS Explorer 441** Access **the walk can
be joined at the end of the golf course from
Golspie via a path along the coastline
(3km); buses and trains to Golspie**

Jutting out into the Loch Fleet estuary
where salt and freshwater meet, this area
has quite rightly been designated a
National Nature Reserve. This route offers
great opportunities for spotting wading
birds, common seals, deer and pine marten
as well as the varied flora for which the
reserve has become known. A good variety
of coast, woodland and mountain views
make this a rewarding circuit.

Take the minor Littleferry road south
from Golspie; there is a parking layby on
the left opposite the pedestrian entrance
to Balblair Wood. Pass the information
boards and follow the path through the

trees, crossing a wooden bridge. In spring
the wood teems with birdlife and the lucky
or patient may spot a Scottish crossbill, the
only bird species unique to Scotland and
very rarely seen. Easier to spot are the
small grey and white crested tits which
dart about from the lower branches.

When paths meet at a crossroads with a
carved seating area, continue straight
ahead. Keep left when the wide track forks
to reach the house at Balblair. Depending
on the state of the tide and footwear, a
choice can be made between crossing the
saltmarsh right beside the water or taking
the path through the woods with glimpses
of the loch. Both join up later on. To take
the path through the woods, follow the red
marker posts past the house, but for the
rougher shore option pass directly in front
of the house towards the water by a faint
path. When three-quarters of the way to
the loch, look for a faint path bearing right
to the pebbly shore and then follow the

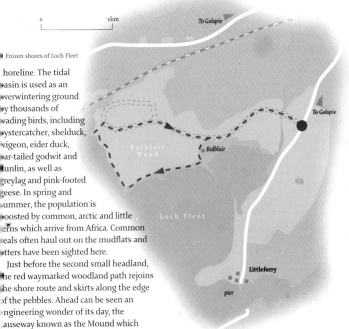

◀ Frozen shores of Loch Fleet

horeline. The tidal
asin is used as an
overwintering ground
y thousands of
wading birds, including
ystercatcher, shelduck,
vigeon, eider duck,
ar-tailed godwit and
unlin, as well as
reylag and pink-footed
eese. In spring and
ummer, the population is
oosted by common, arctic and little
ems which arrive from Africa. Common
eals often haul out on the mudflats and
tters have been sighted here.

Just before the second small headland,
he red waymarked woodland path rejoins
he shore route and skirts along the edge
of the pebbles. Ahead can be seen an
ngineering wonder of its day, the
auseway known as the Mound which
arries the busy A9. Built by Thomas
elford in 1816, the design incorporates
nassive sluice gates to enable the tide to
ush through twice a day and also to allow
assage to migrating trout and salmon.

Round a corner and cross a large bay,
eeping a careful eye out for a red
waymarked path heading inland about
nalfway across. Take this path until it
eaches a track and then turn right through
oung Scots pine trees. Keep a look out for
ine marten, although in daylight you are
nore likely to see their distinctive
troppings. Returning at dawn or dusk

(either with or without the fabled jam
sandwich to lure them!) will give you the
greatest chance of spotting these creatures.
In spring and summer, it is the flowers
that most excite ecologists. Three flowers
link this site to others at the same latitude
in different countries – creeping ladies
tresses, twinflower and the one-flowered
wintergreen which is also known as St
Olaf's candlestick. Ninety percent of the
UK's specimens of this plant grow here.
Continue straight ahead at a crossroads
and also at the next fork to return on the
outward path to the parking area.

Dornoch Links and Embo

Distance **8.5km** Time **3 hours**
Terrain **clear paths, tracks and minor roads with optional section along the beach** Map **OS Explorer 441**
Access **bus and train services to Dornoch**

Examine the fine buildings of the historic Royal Burgh of Dornoch before setting out across the championship golf course to follow an often bracing coastal route to the pier at Embo. The sandy shoreline provides even more variety for the return route.

The main square in Dornoch showcases some of the historic buildings of this fine small town. Built from the local honey-coloured sandstone, the mix includes the old police station and town jail, Dornoch Castle – originally built as the bishop's palace, but now a hotel – and the courthouse. Begin the walk along Bridge Street which heads north alongside a small burn. Cross the road just before the old station building and ascend steps into the wood, signed for Embo. Keep on the path to the left, with the fence on your left as you skirt a house and, after a kissing gate, cross a road to take a woodland path ahead.

Keep following the signs for Embo, turning left and then right to skirt along the edge of a field and then reach an area of gorse. Go straight ahead at a fork to reach the Cholera Grave, dating back to 1832 when the body of a man was brought to Dornoch for burial. Thousands were dying of the disease throughout the country and the people of Dornoch refused entry to the corpse in order to stave off the

disease, so the man was buried at this spot just outside the town.

Just past the gravestone, turn left at a yellow marker to reach the Earl's Cross, a large stone erected to mark the boundary between the lands of the Earl of Sutherland and those belonging to the Church. The stone shows the shields of both the Earl and the Bishop of Caithness. Keep on the main route, ignoring the path towards the sea and golf course. When you meet the old railway line, carry on along this to reach a large white house. Immediately after this, turn right along a stony track.

Cross a stile by a gate and follow the track to the golf course. At the far end of the course, pass through a metal and then a wooden gate and take the grassy path towards Embo. At the edge of the caravan park, cross the burn and turn right along the shore path to reach the pier, battered by the North Sea waves.

To return, either retrace your steps as far as the golf course or instead cross the sands to reach the path at the edge of the course. Now keep to the route

marked by red posts along the seaward edge of the course, which briefly joins a track. When the track crosses the course, stay on the grassy path at the left-hand edge. The track returns again and leads to the southern end of the course. From here, head towards the car park and lifeboat station, keeping straight on at a T-junction to pass the clubhouse and return to the square in the centre of Dornoch.

caravan park

Embo pier

Embo Street

old railway line

golf course

0   1km

Earl's Cross

golf course

Dornoch

cathedral   Dornoch Square

◂ Foam on Dornoch beach

Dornoch Point

Distance **6.5km** Time **2 hours 30**
Terrain **rough and indistinct paths
through the dunes, sandy beach**
Map **OS Explorer 438** Access **bus and train
services to Dornoch**

**Experience the wilder side of Dornoch on
this walk along the coast to the Point, the
haunt of seabirds and seals. Return via a
peaceful meander through the dunes,
leaving time to enjoy the combined
pleasures of historic buildings and fine
homebaking that Dornoch has to offer.**

Start from the main square in Dornoch
and walk south along Church Street,
following the sign for the beach. After a
short distance, turn left into Carnaig Street
which runs between a row of houses and
their gardens. In the final garden, a small
stone marks the place where the last

person was tried and executed for
witchcraft. The macabre incident occurred
in 1727 when both Janet Horne, an elderly
woman who may have been suffering from
dementia, and her daughter were
convicted of being witches. One of the
crimes for which Janet stood accused was
that of turning her daughter into a horse
and getting Satan to shoe the creature.
After the conviction, the daughter escaped
but Janet was stripped, rolled in tar and
paraded through the town in a barrel
before being burnt to death. The capital
offence of witchcraft was repealed in 1735.

Turn right and then immediately left to
follow the road beside the golf course. Go
through the entrance to the caravan park,
keeping to the right to cross a bridge and
accompany a track to the end of the site.
From here, bear left through the dunes;

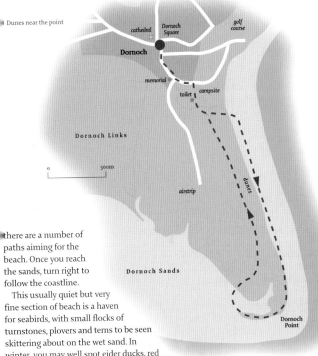

Dunes near the point

there are a number of
paths aiming for the
beach. Once you reach
the sands, turn right to
follow the coastline.

This usually quiet but very
fine section of beach is a haven
for seabirds, with small flocks of
turnstones, plovers and terns to be seen
skittering about on the wet sand. In
winter, you may well spot eider ducks, red
throated divers and common scoters on
the water. As the far end of the beach
draws near, the tall Tarbet Ness Lighthouse
looms ahead, and Tain can be seen across
the water as the point is rounded. If the
tide is high, you'll need to keep to the edge
of the dunes to Dornoch Point.

Continue around the corner until the
dunes merge into saltmarsh. Here, a faint

path heads inland, keeping between the
marsh and the dunes. Keep aiming for the
buildings of Dornoch; there are a number
of different paths, but most converge at
the corner of the caravan park passed
earlier in the walk. From here, retrace the
route through the caravan park and back
up Carnaig Street to the centre of Dornoch.

75

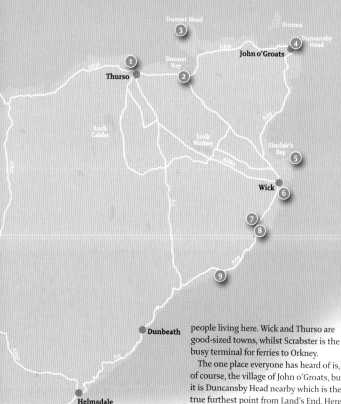

The most northeasterly part of Scotland contrasts starkly with the vast neighbouring county of Sutherland. Apart from its southern fringe, Caithness lacks mountains and, although parts of it may be wild and empty, there are far more people living here. Wick and Thurso are good-sized towns, whilst Scrabster is the busy terminal for ferries to Orkney.

The one place everyone has heard of is, of course, the village of John o'Groats, but it is Duncansby Head nearby which is the true furthest point from Land's End. Here stand two magnificent sea stacks, giving a clue to one of Caithness' best-loved attractions, its coastline of mighty cliffs and wide sandy bays. The landscape is also rich in history, with fine castles dotted all along the coastline and scores of remarkable prehistoric remains, including the amazing Grey Cairns of Camster.

Wick Harbour ▶

Caithness

Holborn Head

Distance 7.5km Time 2 hours
Terrain very high clifftop paths, faint in
places, farm track and road with
pavement; a long, steep flight of steps
near the return can be avoided by a detour
Map OS Explorer 451 Access bus (X99) from
Inverness via Thurso

Starting from Scrabster, the ferry terminal
for Orkney, this walk passes the
lighthouse built to guide the ferries and
fishing vessels to safety. It leads out to
Holborn Head with its impressive cliffs
and explores the coastline beyond, before
returning overland to the harbour.
A shorter walk is possible by returning
straight back from Holborn Head.

It is possible to park at Scrabster Harbour
or you can catch the bus or take the clifftop
footpath from Thurso. To begin the walk,
follow the road from Scrabster Fishermen's
Mission towards the ferry terminal,
passing the long stay car park. Keep on the
left side of the road to head towards the
lighthouse. The lighthouse, which was, like
almost all those in Scotland, built by the
Stevenson family, was discontinued in
2003, but it still provides a welcome
landmark to the ships heading in and out
of the port. Hoy, one of the nearest Orkney
islands to the mainland, can be seen
straight ahead, but the ferries bypass this
en route to the port at Stromness on the
Orkney mainland, as the largest of the
group is called. In the past, this route was
popular as a staging post for the Norsemen
who ruled much of the area. The name
Holborn derives from the Norse and
means 'Hill fort'. Just before reaching the
lighthouse, turn up to the left through a
gate signed for Holborn Head.

The route climbs steeply and, after
passing the garden wall of the lightkeeper's
house, aims diagonally right on a vague
path. After crossing a stile and as it
approaches the cairn on the headland itself
the path soon improves. Concrete planks
ease the crossing of a number of small

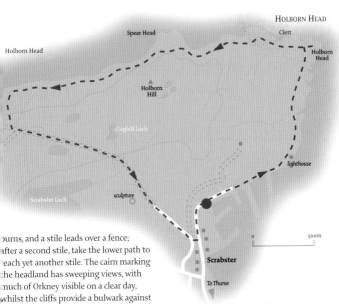

Holborn Head

Spear Head

Clett

Holborn
Head

Holborn Head

Holborn
Hill

Coghill Loch

lighthouse

Scrabster Loch

sculpture

Scrabster

To Thurso

burns, and a stile leads over a fence;
after a second stile, take the lower path to
reach yet another stile. The cairn marking
the headland has sweeping views, with
much of Orkney visible on a clear day,
whilst the cliffs provide a bulwark against
the battering waves during storms.

The next section of the walk allows a
proper appreciation of the awesome
sandstone cliffs along this part of the
coast. From the cairn, return a little way
along the path to a fork and bear right,
taking care near the cliff edge. Soon a
natural arch and blowhole is reached
where the sea is sometimes forced up to
make an impressive explosion of spray.
The local word for these collapsed sea
caves is *gloup* from the Norse word for
'throat'; their existence makes you realise
that the cliffs you are walking on are
probably riddled with deep sea caves –
hopefully with stronger ceilings!

Keep to the faint path around the coast.
After Robertson's Point, a high sea stack

with an arch can be seen. The path goes
through two gates in fences as it works its
way around the coast and eventually
reaches a series of jutting cliffs known as
the Turrets. Continue until the way is
blocked by a deep geo, or inlet. Accompany
the fence inland from here, turning right
through a gate and then immediately left
through a farm gate to follow the track
across barren moorland. After some
distance, pass through a farm gate
(sometimes locked) and by a building as
the track descends to Scrabster. Go straight
ahead on the road and, at the parking area
at the top of the hill, walk diagonally left to
reach the top of a long flight of concrete
steps leading to the harbour. At the bottom,
turn left to return to the start of the walk.

Caithness Flagstone Trail

Distance 3.75km **Time** 1 hour 30
Terrain straightforward paths, track and
minor road **Map** OS Explorer 451
Access bus (80, 81, 181, X99) from Thurso
to Castletown; follow signs from main
street for Heritage Centre

Caithness sandstone was once a booming
industry; it splits easily to make regular
flagstones and many of the buildings,
roofs and field boundaries are made from
the sandy-coloured rock. This walk
combines a sculpture trail with an
informative heritage trail which weaves
between old quarries and stone yards to
the quay from which the stone was
exported all over the world.

Castletown lies between Thurso and
John o'Groats on the A836. From the town
centre, take the road to the north signed
for the Heritage Trail, which soon reaches a
car park on the left. An information board
at the opposite corner from the heritage
centre marks the start of the walk. The trail
has been built on land used for quarrying
Caithness sandstone since 1793. Follow the
path uphill through the trees, detouring
first to the right to view the first flagstone
sculpture and then across the main path to
reach a group of carved animals. Climb to
the sculpture of a family group before
joining the main path again, opposite a
large slab artwork. Turn right and return to
the car park.

The route now heads to the coast to visit
a Victorian cannon battery. Cross the car
park and this time take the track lined with
flagstones. At a bend, bear right to reach
the coast and keep to the track with its
great views across the bay to Dunnet Head,
the most northerly point on the British
mainland. The wave-cut platform of rock
below is popular with seabirds, including
terns and ringed plovers; look out for
inquisitive bobbing seals in the water
beyond. A grassy hummock on the left is

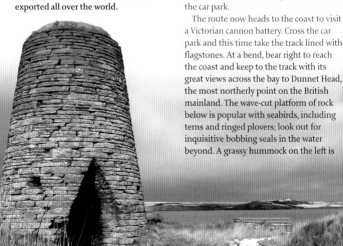

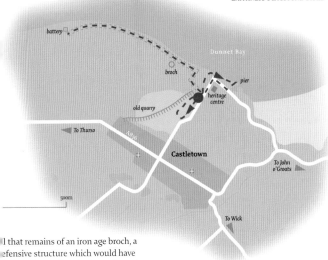

...l that remains of an iron age broch, a ...efensive structure which would have ...een used as a refuge in times of attack ...om the sea.

...After passing some concrete buildings, ...e cannon battery can be seen ahead. Now ...ccupied by sheep and inaccessible to ...alkers, it was originally used by a local ...olunteer regiment set up in 1866 as a ...recursor to the modern-day Territorial ...rmy. Although the regiment never saw ...ctive service, it provided a stream of ...ecruits to the regular army and was also ...alled upon to perform gun salutes for ...oyal events and other occasions.

...Return along the track until you're ...lmost at the car park, but before entering ...urn left through a gate to follow the ...lagstone Trail. Interpretive boards tell the ...tory of the once thriving quarry and stone ...rocessing plants that employed more ...han 500 people at the end of the 1800s.

The route passes the windmill used to power the stone-cutting saws, after which the rock would be polished and hauled along tracks by horses to the harbour to be loaded onto ships for export.

The path winds between the remains before bearing right and heading down to the beautiful harbour, built from vertically positioned stones to give it strength against the battering seas. Here, you'll see seats and poles used for drying fishing nets. Although the flagstone industry declined rapidly after the introduction of concrete and cheaper imports, Caithness stone is still highly valued today and the industry remains important, though on a much smaller scale. From the harbour, follow the road back to the car park, passing the heritage centre.

Remains of the windmill

Dunnet Head

Distance **17km** Time **6 hours 30**
Terrain **this walk is much tougher than
most others in this book; much of the
ground has a faint path, but it is very
rough and boggy, often steep and with
unprotected cliff edges nearby; good
navigation and hillwalking skills and
equipment needed** Map OS Explorer 451
Access **bus (80) from Thurso and John
o'Groats to Dunnet, 500m from start**

Approaching the most northerly point of
the British mainland on foot is
challenging, but makes one of the most
dramatic walks in Caithness. This circuit
offers superb clifftop scenery,
unsurpassed views towards Hoy and the
other Orkney islands and a feast of
birdwatching opportunities. The walk can
be shortened if a lift is arranged from
Dunnet Head Lighthouse.

Start at Dwarwick Pier, which can be
reached from the A836 by turning off
through Dunnet and then going left at the
T-junction past Mary Ann's Cottage; there

is a parking and picnic area at the pier.
From here, a clear path whisks you north,
through a kissing gate and straight up the
steep hillside; ignore a path further left
that leads only to a cliff edge. After this
energetic start, the ground levels off into
rough moorland. The path is a little way
back from the high cliffs and soon
descends to a bay with a sandy beach,
accessible only from the sea. Pass the ruin
of a house before climbing once more over
a rise. Follow the coastline at a safe
distance, passing behind two inlets or geo
where the sea pounds into a weakness in
the rock and birds seek sheltered nesting
spots on the sheer sides.

Cross one outflow from the Loch of
Bushta before reaching a second which has
carved The Thirl, a dramatic geo, where it
meets the sea. Just beyond is Chapel Geo,
though the chapel itself is now little more
than a pile of stones. Another steep and
pathless climb has to be tackled which
requires great care because of the
unprotected drop to the left; it is safer to

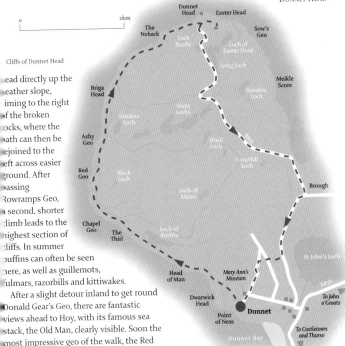

Cliffs of Dunnet Head

ead directly up the
eather slope,
iiming to the right
f the broken
ocks, where the
ath can then be
ejoined to the
eft across easier
ground. After
assing
Rowramps Geo,
a second, shorter
climb leads to the
highest section of
cliffs. In summer
puffins can often be seen
here, as well as guillemots,
fulmars, razorbills and kittiwakes.

After a slight detour inland to get round
Donald Gear's Geo, there are fantastic
views ahead to Hoy, with its famous sea
stack, the Old Man, clearly visible. Soon the
most impressive geo of the walk, the Red
Geo, is reached and, afterwards, Dunnet
Head Lighthouse can be seen across
Sanders Loch.

More clifftop scenery leads to the Long
Byre, a great trench probably formed when
a cave collapsed; pass around it to the right
before the final approach to the
lighthouse. Keep right where the path
forks to emerge onto the road, and then
turn left to visit the lighthouse. It is worth
accompanying the track off to the right to
visit the nearby trig point, which has the
best views. Afterwards, head back down

the road, passing Long Loch and finally
nearing the coast at Brough. Here, turn
right, following the sign for Thurso. After
2km, look for a grassy path to the right,
soon after a left-hand bend. This path
leads to a road; dog-leg left and then right
across it onto another path and then turn
left at the next two T-junctions before a
right turn onto the public road brings you
back past Mary Ann's Cottage and the road
to Dwarwick Pier.

Duncansby Head from John o'Groats

Distance 8.5km **Time** 3 hours
Terrain faint grassy paths with some
boggy sections and an area of sandy
shoreline; care needed near cliff edges
Map OS Explorer 451 **Access** buses from
Thurso (80) and Wick (77)

Escape the tourist bustle of John o'Groats
to follow the coastline and discover the
true most northeasterly point in Britain.
With great views to Orkney and a fine
lighthouse, the best is yet to come when
you venture along the clifftop to the
hidden highlights of Duncansby, with
amazing sea stacks, arches and deep
inlets, all humming with seabirds and salt
spray from the waves far below.

There is a large car park at John o'Groats,
with its variety of shops, cafés and a tiny
museum. Whilst this is a destination in
itself for many, especially the hundreds of
weary cyclists and charity runners who
make the 1407km (874-mile) journey from
Land's End in Cornwall, the real gem is
further along the coast near Duncansby
Head itself.

Begin by walking down to the harbour
and passing two huge Caithness stone
slabs on the right, which mark the start of
the path. Skirt around the back of the
beach, then climb the grassy bank and go
through two kissing gates and over a small
bridge. The path crosses the back of a bay
known as Robert's Haven, passing an old

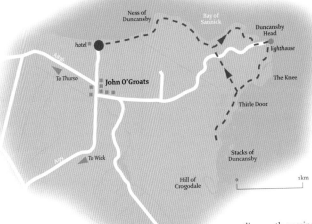

Ness of
Duncansby

Bay of
Sannick

Duncansby
Head

hotel

lighthouse

To Thurs

The Knee

John O'Groats

Thirle Door

To Wick

Stacks of
Duncansby

Hill of
Crogodale

0   1km

Biel of
Duncansby

winch used for hauling fishing boats up above the tideline. Aim for a wooden post at the Ness of Duncansby, where there is a seat with a good view of the swirling, usually angry waters of the Pentland Firth which separate the mainland from Orkney.

The next beach is the Bay of Sannick; after crossing a burn near the far end, there is a steep ascent up the grassy slope towards a stile. Keep well back from the cliff edge to pass the Glupe, a massive blowhole. From here, head directly up to the road and turn left to reach Duncansby Head Lighthouse. Although Dunnet Head is further north, this is the northeasternmost point on the British mainland and the views out to Orkney are superb. However, the real highlight of the area, the great Stacks, are still out of sight.

Take the signed path just before the lighthouse which soon follows the coastline south, passing the Geo of Sclaites, a dramatic, vertically-sided inlet. The Stacks are now in view, two spectacular pyramids of rock, with a natural arch, Thirle Door, as a foreground. After crossing a boggy depression, the cliff path rises until you are directly opposite the Stacks. During the months of May, June and July the Stacks and cliffs are dotted with white, a swirling mass of seabirds which nest on the more sheltered rockfaces, providing free entertainment to the visitors.

From here, return to the boggy depression and take the faint, grassy track which aims directly for the the lighthouse road, reaching it at the point where the Burn of Sannick runs down to the shore. Cross the road and head down to Sannick Bay on the left side of the burn. Pick up the outward route here and retrace your steps along the coast.

◀ The Stacks of Duncansby

Noss Head and Castle Sinclair Girnigoe

Distance 9km **Time** 3 hours
Terrain rough coastal walking with
unprotected cliffs and faint paths; farm
tracks and minor roads on return
Map OS Explorer 450 **Access** bus (76) from
Wick to Staxigoe, or you can walk along
the road or coastal path from Wick

Follow the coast from the harbour at
Staxigoe to enjoy spectacular clifftop
scenery en route to the lighthouse at Noss
Head. The extensive ruins of Castle
Sinclair Girnigoe are perched high above
the sea near here and provide a
fascinating objective for the walk.

Staxigoe is a small village which grew up
as a result of the clearing of tenants from

the inland straths to make way for sheep.
Situated just north of Wick, the harbour
and surrounding Caithness stone-built
buildings once comprised one of the
busiest herring stations in Europe with
more than 50 boats hauling in the herring
to be gutted, salted and placed in barrels
by an army of women. It was then shipped
to England, Ireland and the Baltic states, as
well as the Americas where it was used to
feed the slave populations. Herring was
also smoked locally to produce kippers;
both herring and kippers made up the
staple diet of the inhabitants of this area
until the end of the herring boom.

There is limited parking near the harbour
at Staxigoe. From here, pass the harbour

and continue north along a lane, passing through the farmyard of Noss Farm to reach a gate into a field. Follow the fence along the right-hand edge of the field before climbing a stile to access the clifftop path, which is narrow and unprotected. Ahead, Noss Lighthouse can be seen along a wild stretch of coastline. The path passes a number of small sea stacks and round two deep geos or clefts where seabirds can often be seen clinging to the steep sides.

Eventually, the lighthouse boundary wall comes into view. Head diagonally towards it, aiming for the gate, and then on towards the lighthouse. Before reaching it, another gate leads to the access road; turn left here to leave the lighthouse and reach the parking area. The impressive ruins of Castle Sinclair Girnigoe are reached by making a detour down to the end of a track, which begins opposite the car park. The castle stands high above the waves on a stack between two deep geos. Built in the late 15th century, it has been a ruin for the last 300 years. The ruins are open only from May to September, but there are good views of the castle from the path at other times. A long-term renovation project aims to restore much of the building and use archaeology to uncover the clues to its history, much of which remains unknown.

Return to the lighthouse parking area and turn right to follow the road inland. At the crossroads, turn left; Wick airport is directly ahead. The road turns sharp left again at the outskirts of Staxigoe, before leading down to the harbour and back to the start.

◄ Noss Head coastline

Wick and Old Castle

Distance 6.5km **Time** 2 hours **Terrain** good paths or pavement; care is needed near the castle itself which has unprotected cliffs **Map** OS Explorer 450 **Access** Wick is well served by buses and trains

Explore modern-day Wick, together with evidence of its much older heritage, including the harbour, once a seething mass of herring boats, and the Old Castle, now a clifftop ruin but once the mainland Scottish stronghold for the King of Norway in the 12th century.

Start from the centre of Wick. There is ample parking in the riverside car park next to the supermarket. Take the road opposite the supermarket entrance, passing the public toilets and reaching the main A99 at the top of the road. Turn right onto this and then use the crossing to go straight ahead onto Wick High Street where the main A99 road turns sharply right. Follow the High Street to the far end and cross

over the river, then turn left onto Martha Terrace to head to the harbour.

Wick Harbour is today the heart of a busy industrial port, whilst the inner harbour has a marina for leisure boats. Built by Thomas Telford to house the larger fishing vessels that emerged during the herring boom, it quickly eclipsed nearby Staxigoe as the local fishing hub. Keep on the road to pass two small docks, looking out for the sign for Trinkie Pool. Take this road which slopes uphill to reach Pulteneytown. This part of Wick was created by the British Fisheries Society and named after the governor of the Society at the time, Sir William Pulteney. The lower part was dedicated to the actual fishing and processing of the herring, while the higher ground was used to provide

housing. Old Pulteney Distillery is still located in this part of Wick.

At the top of the hill, turn left next to the post office to follow Smith Terrace which has great views over the harbour and river mouth below. After passing an area of green space, continue to the impressive memorial to James Bremner who built much of the more modern outer harbour. Carry on by the clifftop path and turn left when it emerges onto a road.

Ignore any paths off to the right and pass a concrete building from the Second World War. When you reach the parking area for Wick Old Castle, cross the stile and go through a gate. The castle is almost cut off from the mainland by deep clefts in the coastline. The path bears left after some army buildings and passes between two fences. Ignore the stile straight ahead, instead turning left to reach the castle. Take care on the final approach as it is almost surrounded by vertical drops into the sea.

Once a mighty four-storey tower, the still-impressive castle has been standing on this site since it was built in the 12th century by Harald Maddadson, Earl of Caithness. This was a time when the Norse kingdom included Orkney and Caithness, and this strategically important castle was their chief stronghold on the mainland.

From the castle, return a short way along the path and back around the deep geo. Now head inland, crossing a small bridge and then following a lane across the fields. Keep straight ahead at a crossroads to eventually emerge on the A99. Turn right to walk on the pavement by the main road all the way back to the centre of Wick.

◀ Castle of Old Wick

Yarrows Archaeological Trail

Distance 3.5km **Time** 1 hour 30
Terrain moorland, very wet underfoot,
waterproof boots needed **Map** OS Explorer
450 **Access** bus (75) from Wick and
Helmsdale to Thrumster, 2.5km from start
along minor roads

Follow this waymarked trail over the now
silent moors to visit a fine array of
archaeological sites telling the stories of
the people of long ago.

The Yarrows Archaeological Trail is
signed from the A99 just south of
Thrumster, between Lybster and Wick.
The road weaves through the scattered
houses in this exposed moorland
community before a turn leads eventually
to a parking area at South Yarrows. A leaflet
about the walk is sometimes available from
a dispenser, but the route is waymarked by
wooden posts. Start through the small gate
and go downhill towards the Loch of
Yarrows. After passing through a second
gate, walk down the large field, crossing to
the other side of the fence on the left at
another gate. A final gate brings you to the
clear though tumbledown remains of a
broch. This former defensive tower is
thought to date from 200BC to 200AD. The
hollow walls contained a small guard cell
to protect the entrance, as well as stairs to
the upper floors.

From the broch, return to the large field
and accompany the white posts, parallel to

he loch at first, then
hrough a gap in the fence
n the left. Keep looking
out for the next post,
keeping close to the fence
and then crossing a stile
ahead to reach a group of
faint hut circles amongst
the heather. These were
either iron or bronze age,
dating back 3500 years.
A conical roof would
have been supported by
timbers resting on the
stone circular walls.
Nearby the small lumps
are piles of stones, the result
of many hours clearing areas
for cultivation, an occupation still
familiar to many of today's crofters.

The going gets much wetter underfoot
as the route follows a small ridge, crossing
two stiles as it climbs and eventually
reaches the hilltop crowned by the large
upright piles of stone. Head over to the left
to reach the first of the two Cairns of
Warehouse. These two chambered cairns
are probably neolithic, being up to 5800
years old, and were most likely used for
burials. Cross to the second cairn which
has tall, more recent cairns on top.

Go north from here, descending slightly
and then crossing a stile. Look out for the
standing stone over to the left, and a
further chambered cairn ahead to the right.
The very wet path skirts the right edge of a

rocky mound of heather which is probably
the remains of an iron age hill fort. The
marker posts continue, leading along the
ridge with good views across the loch and
the surrounding moorland. Soon the
collapsed but imposing remains of a large
long cairn are reached, with an obvious
entrance at the near end. Further on are the
remains of a second long cairn; when
excavated in 1853, this was found to
contain a burial, necklace and bronze age
pottery. Far less remains of this cairn,
though the two upright stones on either
side of the entrance are obvious. From the
cairn, turn right to head down to the road
beside the parking area.

◀ Long Cairn, South Yarrows

Whaligoe Steps and the Cairn of Get

Distance 3km **Time** 1 hour 30
Terrain extreme care needed on the very
steep Whaligoe Steps; path to Cairn of
Get has some muddy sections; the walk
crosses the busy A9 **Map** OS Explorer 450
Access bus (75) from Wick and Helmsdale

Two great feats of stone engineering from
different eras combine in this fascinating
walk. The Whaligoe Steps are 330 slabs of
stone clinging spectacularly to the vertical
walls of an otherwise inaccessible
harbour, whilst the nearby Cairn of Get is
a very well-preserved Bronze Age
chambered cairn.

Whaligoe is a row of cottages just south
of Ulbster, between Lybster and Wick on
the A99. From the main road at Whaligoe,
take a minor road heading inland, signed
for the Cairn of Get. There is a small
parking area at the south end of Loch

Watenan (if full there is a car park just past
the Whaligoe cottages on the other side of
the A9). From the Cairn of Get parking,
walk a short distance back along the minor
road and, at the bend before the old
railway cottage, turn right through a
kissing gate.

The route is marked by black and white
posts which lead you along the edge of the
field to another gate. The path then winds
uphill through the gorse bushes; look out
for another kissing gate at the far corner.
Cross the next field on a wooden
boardwalk and climb the stile and slope to
reach a final marker post with the Cairn of
Get just ahead. Approximately 4000 years
old, the long, now open entrance passage
leads to the chamber itself, which would
once have been roofed and used for burial.

From the Cairn of Get, return to the
minor road and continue straight down it

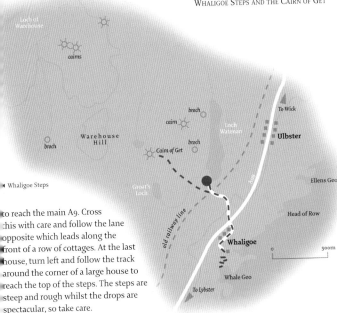

Loch of
Warehouse

cairns

broch

cairn

Loch
Watenan

broch

To Wick

Ulbster

Warehouse
Hill

Cairn of Get

broch

broch

◄ Whaligoe Steps

Groat's
Loch

Ellens Geo

Head of Row

old railway line

A9

Whaligoe

0   500m

Whale Geo

To Lybster

to reach the main A9. Cross
this with care and follow the lane
opposite which leads along the
front of a row of cottages. At the last
house, turn left and follow the track
around the corner of a large house to
reach the top of the steps. The steps are
steep and rough whilst the drops are
spectacular, so take care.

Much of this stretch of coastline is lined
by high, precipitous cliffs, making access to
the sea very difficult. Thomas Telford,
having built the harbour at Wick, came
here in 1786 and declared it to be a 'terrible
spot'. However, the local landowner, David
Brodie, was determined and spent £8 to
have 365 stone steps built. Opening up
access to the sea here proved a good move,
with a regular fleet of 14 boats fishing from
Whaligoe in 1814 and rising to 24 at the
height of the herring boom in 1824. Part
way down, a large flat stone is where the
women, carrying up basket creels packed
with fish on their backs, would rest their
load for a short while before continuing to

the top. The fish was then taken to market
in Wick. Herring was also salted down at
the foot of the steps and exported in
barrels by schooner from the large
platform at the bottom.

The 330 remaining steps are an amazing
testament to man's determination to
overcome the obstacles of nature and also
to the muscle power of the army of women
carrying the heavy baskets of fish up and
the even heavier salt down. More recently,
local people have also shown great
determination with a small group of
volunteers regularly repairing and
maintaining the steps.

Badbea Clearance Village

Distance 2km **Time** 1 hour
Terrain good path to monument and
ruins, rougher path over heather for the
rest of the circuit **Map** OS Explorer 444
Access no public transport

Windswept, precipitous cliffs, poor soil,
no direct access to the sea and no family
connections would not top the list for a
desirable location to build a village.
Badbea has all these features, and yet it
was here that the families cleared from
the neighbouring straths were forced to
set up home. This walk explores the ruins;
the views are stunning on a good day, but
unremittingly bleak otherwise, with
information boards providing clues to a
dark period of history.

The car park for this walk is signed from
the A9, about 7km north of Helmsdale. The
path begins through a gate; where it forks,
go straight ahead and climb over a small
rise. The path then starts a descent
towards the sloping clifftop on which the
settlement of Badbea was hewn from the
heather and peat.

In 1793, more than 80 people, making up
12 families, were forcibly evicted from their
homes in the straths of Langwell, Ousdale
and Berriedale and made to set up home in
this desolate spot. While the more fertile
and sheltered ground was taken for
profitable sheep farming, this area,
hemmed in between a high wall built to
keep the sheep from wandering over the
cliffs, and the cliff edges themselves, could

e spared and was made available to the tenants. With no direct access to the sea, fishing had to be done from Berriedale, further north, under the control of the landowner. There were some jobs available on the estate to bring life to subsistence levels, but wages were low and anyone found working elsewhere was liable to have their family put out of their home by the laird.

Aim first for the large stone monument. This records the names of the residents, the last of whom left in 1911 having been the only inhabitant since 1903. The monument was erected in the same year by David Sutherland, the son of Alexander Sutherland, who had emigrated from Badbea to New Zealand in 1839.

From the monument, as you look out to sea, bear right to reach an information board beside the ruins of several houses. From here, the easier option is to return the same way. If intent on a rougher circuit, turn left and follow a faint path heading north across the slope, passing

more remains and eventually reaching some more substantial ruins where one house still has a stone lintel in place. Looking back from here, the scale of the high cliffs can be seen and, with a cold wind blowing off the sea, the difficulties of living here can begin to be appreciated. Reports claim that the womenfolk would often tether their cattle, hens and even children to stop them being blown off the dangerous cliffs during storms.

From the better preserved ruins, walk left uphill, aiming for a clear gap in the stone wall ahead. Go through this to reach an old track and follow this to the left; it leads all the way back to the car park at the start.

◄ Badbea Monument

Index